Messages from Above

Messages from Above

Bev & Barb Munro

Library of Congress Control Number:		2016903261
ISBN:	Hardcover	978-1-5144-7073-2
	Softcover	978-1-5144-7072-5
	eBook	978-1-5144-7071-8

Printed in Canada

Rev. date: 06/02/2016

To order additional copies of this book, contact:
Xlibris
1-888-795-4274
www.Xlibris.com
Orders@Xlibris.com
732008

To Donna

To a very gentle kind
soul who has the most
giving heart

Bill & Barb

BEV'S FOREWORD

As I sit and ponder the miraculous gift of being able to channel messages, I also realize this is a gift available for all of God's creatures. It is a gift that he wants all his creatures to experience, so the simplest ways to channel messages is just by asking the question and waiting for the answer.

Don't be afraid to pick up a pen and paper and begin writing. You will find that you begin with gibberish, but as you continue writing, eventually you will begin to channel beautiful messages for yourself and others.

You will find a door has opened that brings you peace and serenity; you will receive the answers you have struggled to find for years.

I encourage you all to begin to trust that God answers all your questions; you just need to understand what vessel God provides you as your means to find the solutions to your daily trials. It may be through the art of writing, it might be placed on your heart, or the answer may come as simply as whispers in your ear, but know that God does answer every question.

BARB'S FOREWORD

As I follow in the steps of my older sister (fifteen minutes), I am thrilled to receive the same gift as her—the same gift that is available for everyone reading this book. I started by setting aside some time every day to just scribble, the way I did as a child pretending I could write. I would scribble on pages and pages of a notebook wondering how this could ever result in the gift of receiving messages from God.

One night as I was in my back bedroom scribbling away, my sister called. I asked her, "Do you have soft spiritual music playing and a candle burning when you receive your messages?"

She told me, "No, I have to have complete silence. I prefer it if no one is home, and even then, I have to have all the bedroom doors closed as to ensure no noise is coming from these rooms. Also, I have to have a clean house."

I immediately turned off the music, blew out the candle, and continued with my scribbling. That was the evening I received my first message.

I encourage anyone reading this book to try the same technique with patience and vigilance, and I believe you will be rewarded with *messages from above.*

Dear Lord Jesus,

Do you have a message for my good friend Josie?

* * *

Dear Josie,

I am always with you. Reach out and feel me beside you. I never leave your side. Call out to me, and I will answer. Just like your friend Barb, you too can hear me; you too can communicate with me. Try and you will see how easy it is to have a relationship with me.

You wonder about your son Carter, the beat of your heart. Yes, it is true we love the difficult ones just a little bit more, because if their mother does not love them, who will? Carter is very sad. Carter does not know where his life is going. Carter has yet to find his place in this hard and cold world. For Carter, it is hard and cold, with little love, little success, and only disappointment and bitterness.

You ask, is Carter a sociopath? No! Carter has the capability to love; he adores his little girl. He is just a lost soul that cannot find his place here on planet Earth. Pray for your son, Josie. Pray for the peace that passes all understanding. Pray that your son finds his place in life.

You ask, why doesn't he reply to my e-mails and multiple phone calls? Carter is embarrassed. Carter does not want his mother to know what a mess he has made of his life. Carter feels like he is a failure, thirty-six years old and nothing to show for all his hard work. He has tried to make his marriage work and tries very hard to be a good dad, but feels like he is failing at both. What does your son need from you?

Love, Josie. Carter needs your love, the unconditional love of a mother. How, you ask. How can I show my son love when I never see him? Send him love. Ask your angels to take love to him wherever he is. Love him from a distance; continue to send your love letters via e-mail. Love, love, love—that is what your son needs!

Your precious baby girl—yes Josie, you still think of her as your baby girl. Is she happier than Carter? Slightly, she too struggles with feeling like a failure. She too needs your love, different from Carter in that you can tell her how much you love her. She loves it when you tell her stories of when she was a little girl. Think of a different story to tell her each time you talk. Make it your mission to think of a different little girl story to tell your baby each time you talk.

Think of a funny little story to e-mail Carter each day, ending your correspondence with "Carter, my precious son, you are the beat of my heart, and I love you more than life itself."

Your precious Nathan—yes, your firstborn and perfect child. Is he happy? It may be stretching it a little to say that he is happy, but he is content and does not feel the same sense of failure that your other children feel.

Josie, you were a great mom, and Michelle and Carter's feelings of failure have nothing to do with your parenting. You set a wonderful example of hard work, commitment, and love for all three of your children. Did Dennis have anything to do with Carter and Michelle's station in life? You ask. No! Dennis is just a good punching bag to blame their own mistakes on. These children were grown—even Michelle at fifteen was a woman who made up her own mind by the time you married Dennis.

Each one of us has a path to walk in life. Each one of us has a journey to take. Life lessons to learn. Carter chose to learn about unconditional love, and he has certainly challenged everyone in his life to see how far that unconditional love would carry him. Now he must learn to show unconditional love to a daughter that will challenge him throughout his life here on planet Earth. Carter has much to learn yet, and his hardest lessons are to come.

BEV & BARB MUNRO

Your beautiful Michelle chose to learn about hardship. We learn best from hardship, and needless to say, she is learning a lot. The life she has chosen is a very hard way to live life on this planet called Earth, but she is adding hardship to her life by causing financial difficulties for herself.

Do not help Michelle out with money. Let her learn the lesson she has chosen. Continue to let her know that you love her, but do not give her money.

Your precious angel Ava—yes, you will get to see her. Yes, you will spend much time with her.

Believe this letter, Josie, for everything I tell you is true. Let go of guilt. You have nothing to feel guilty about. Let go of control, for in reality, you control nothing. Let go, let go, let go, and only love. Do you feel it entering your body? Hang on to this feeling, and when you are at your lowest, revisit this feeling and fill your body with love.

Love your son Carter even more right now. Love your daughter Michelle even more right now. Love your son Nathan even more right now, and watch as your life changes. Only love—no resentment, no bitterness, and all your children will come home to their mother, right where they belong.

Remember, I am always with you and want you to ask for help.

Your heavenly Father,

My dear, Precious Lord, do you have a message for my friend Deidre this morning? A message of hope, a message of love?

* * *

Dear Deidre,

Let the tears fall, my child. Let the tears fall, for when the tears fall, the sadness leaks out with them. Oh, Deidre, your greatest sorrow, your son Levi. What is wrong with him? you ask. What is wrong with a son that can treat his mother like this?

Levi is a lost soul who doesn't know where he belongs. He doesn't feel like he belongs anywhere. Always Levi has struggled with wondering where he belongs. He belongs to me the *Lord God*, but he doesn't know that. He shoos away my presence, he shoos away my love, and now he has nowhere to belong. He does not feel like he belongs to this birth family, he does not feel like he belongs to the family he married into, and he is not sure he even belongs to his daughter.

It is a very lonely world when you have no place of belonging, and Levi is a very lonely boy. Why does he push you away if he is so lonely? He is embarrassed. He does not want to get caught in a lie by his mother, of all people.

Deidre, never think that your son does not love you. Levi loves you the best way he knows how, and you are right, "he sure as hell does not know how very well."

Your son is a ball of pain, a ball of rejection, and a ball of sorrow. He feels lost and alone, and please don't let the actions of a lost and alone little boy stop you from showing him love. Your son receives love from nowhere else than his mother. Take a break if you must, but then remember your Levi when he was your little boy. Do you remember a time when he felt lost and alone? Do you remember your little boy when his dad left him? Your son still carries the pain of when his dad left him, as do your other two children.

Deidre, love this lost and alone little boy, take a small break from your love messages, take care of you for a short while, but always be the mother. Always show your love to the son who feels love from no other source. He does not mean to hurt you, but when a person is so full of hurt, it is inevitable that he will hurt others.

Please, Deidre, do not take this personally. Please, Deidre, know that your son's purpose was not to hurt you but to protect him. Treat your son the way you always wanted to be treated by your parents and that is with unconditional love.

Your Heavenly Father

Dear Precious Lord, Alana is so tormented over her precious son, a gift from you. He is so lonely, feeling so alone and lost, and just wants to come home. Oh, Lord, could you please guide her as to what her role is and what Blair will need to find himself? Praise you, Lord!

* * *

Dearest Beverley,

Alana is tormented over what is best for Blair, what his future holds, where she should turn to for support. She wants answers, and she wants God to work in Blair's life now to end his despair and his unhappiness. The hardest thing a mother ever has to do is watch a child suffer. She feels all his pain, and she, like all mothers, wants to carry this burden. She believes she could carry it easier, and she is right. She could carry it easier than Blair can. A child born of love and a child born of fear, he is trying to find the purpose of his life but is also afraid to find the purpose of his life. Fear is crippling, and at this time, Blair is crippled with his own fear of being homeless, alone, and abandoned. He has great fears of not having anyone in his life that cares. He needs to be loved and needed, and he is now feeling like he isn't loveable, nor is he supported as he struggles to come to grips with his life. Very lost, very scared, and very *lonely* as he works toward being able to determine how his life should proceed, he is caught between the glamour and the security. He's sure the glamour will bring him his happiness, yet he's craving the security of being at home, protected, loved, supported, admired—all the things he needs to bring him his ability to survive. He so wants to make his parents proud. He so wants to make his siblings respect him. He so wants the approval of his grandmother. But how can he possibly do this when he has wasted so many years? How is he ever going to be able to support himself, let alone pay people back? He is such a young boy at heart, just wanting his parents to solve all his problems just like they used to by getting him out of jams and always being available to protect him.

Blair needs protection from his enemies, his enemies being his ability to sabotage all and any good in his life as he prepares to do battle with his demons. He is having trouble seeing the light. His demons never leave him, as they come in the form of severe indecisiveness; they come in the form of the need for glory.

Blair wants all that he does not have and wants not what he already has. He has yet to understand that in God's world, the material means nothing, and there is no room to clutter what God shares with material things. He is about what the spirit and the soul can learn. He is about how the body supports the soul and how the soul supports the body.

Alana, you are the mother God gave to this child—a child that would need much understanding, much love, and much support until he has found his way—and there was nothing accidental about that. Yes, this is taking longer than what you suspected, but it is on God's schedule. It is as he planned, and yes, it is also as Blair planned. Give this son much, and give this son all as he searches for all that awaits him.

And you are his shining star. You are the star that lights his way. You are the strength that keeps him supported. You are the voice that uplifts him. You are the mother that loves him, believes in him, supports him through his mistakes as he searches for that path to righteousness. Don't compare him to your other children. Do not let anyone compare him to his siblings. He was made different to do different things, and these reasons have not been completely revealed, but as he lends his ear to young adults, as he guides them to the path of their choosing, as he is the lead in the life of young searching, his purpose will become clear. There will be more understanding, and the years that went before him will fade away for all those with thoughts of unease for your precious child given to you from God on Mother's Day for a very special reason. This child will always need this mother. She will remain a vital support source and his inspiration. She will remain his purpose to continue his search and his purpose for achieving.

You will see great changes in your son. Believe that this will come to pass through the belief and never-wavering love and recognition he has received from his mom. You are his mom, and love him well. Know that this man will come into his own fruition and will make every attempt possible to give back *all* that you have ever given him as he moves to fill God's plan for him.

Dear Precious Lord, a question for you regarding a Bible passage, John 3:16, "For God so loved the world that he gave his only begotten son for whosoever believeth in him shall not perish but have everlasting life." The question is, what happens to those who don't believe your son is our savior? Praise you for your love, and praise you for your truth. Amen.

* * *

Beverley, a question that brings many answers, a question asked by many, a question that is meant to bring understanding, not confusion, and yet so many are confused, so many frustrated, and so many uncaring of God's love—a love so strong he sent his Son to save the world, knowing that his only Son would have to sacrifice his life in order to bring freedom and deliverance to the world, and yet so many do not believe that this Son is the Son of God. So many do not understand his purpose and his meaning, they choose to believe that God's Son was just an ordinary man, when in fact, God made his Son in his image: the image of love, the image of his own shadow, the image of what he wanted the world to see—the image that all can be obtained through the power of love. All can be obtained through the glory of God; that God cares for his people; that he is full of empathy, compassion, and full of love as he tries to make his children know that life is made up of love; that love is the cycle of the universe; that love brings pain and it takes it away; that Jesus was all-loving as God is all-loving; and that in this image, Jesus is like his Father—the Father that brings the sunshine, the Father that brings the moon, the Father that brings the rains, and the Father that brings all that sustains us, all that carries us, all that brings the harmony of the world.

Jesus is all of this and more, much more. Jesus brought wisdom to the world, the wisdom to learn all that God wants to be shared, the ability to hear the sounds of the earth, the ability to see the sights of the earth, and the ability to bring love to the world. Long after his death, Jesus still brings love to the world. He is able to be the provider to the needs of the people, he is able to be the carrier for the thoughts of the people, and he is able to be the foundation for the love of the people. Although you may consider this to be small, in all of this, Jesus, Son of God, brings the evolution of love, the creation of love, and the meaning of love to all who believe in him.

Jesus, Son of God—trust that he will sit on the right side of his Father, and he will judge the living and the dead as he determines the value, purpose, and destination as all pass through the gates of heaven. He is a fair judge. He is a loving judge. A judge that does not punish, a judge that does not threaten, nor does he persuade, but a judge who is concerned with their moral belief, their kindness, their authority, and their being, and he is also available to show all the purpose of love as they enter the kingdom of heaven. God knows all his people. He knows their beliefs, he knows their hearts, and he knows what has been decided and what comes before and what comes after. He knows the plans of all his people and allows for many mistakes as each comes to know God.

This Bible passage is meant to bring people to God and to bring people to his Son. It is meant to be the loving purpose of his Son, but it is not meant to condemn, for all become the children of God, created by him and returned to him as he prepares all for their life destiny and purpose, it changes and it fluctuates, *but* all comes from God and all returns to God.

Dear Precious Lord, how does prayer change things? How does it make a difference when this life has been preplanned?

* * *

Dearest Beverley, you must know that prayer is God's line of communication with you and with all. Take the time to talk to God. Prayer is meant to bring your concerns, your worries, and your anxieties to God. Prayer is meant to bring your joys, your happiness, and your love to God. Prayer is meant to be able to bring all your fear to God.

Prayer is meant to bring each the ease and faith that God wants all his children to feel. Prayer is meant to allow an opening, a channel, and a relationship to our Lord, our Creator, and our Planner. God wants all his children to partake in conversation with him for he is able to bring much in return for prayer. God is able to bring love through his response to prayer. God is able to bring harmony through his response to prayer. God is able to bring contentment, ease of fear or worry, ease of pain and regret, ease of jealousy and betrayal. God is able to bring the ease of sins and the feelings associated with sin, for through prayer, God brings forgiveness, he allows forgiveness, and he allows for hope to surface. Through prayer, God brings each of his creatures all they crave. It might be understanding or recognition, it might be appreciation or restoration, it might be a need to feel loved or cared for, or it might just be to feel thanked for all the love you heap on your Lord, but for each individual, God provides their needs and provides their wants through prayer.

Prayer has many purposes, it has many benefits, and it brings much comfort necessary to live what has been planned. Life on earth becomes hard. It becomes part of what brings his creatures many hardships and many tears as they work toward understanding their purpose, a hard lesson, a lesson that is left unlearned by so many as they struggle to be all that they are meant to be in this lifetime. Through prayer, God brings them the courage to continue. Through prayer, God brings them the hope to continue. And through prayer, God allows them the belief that all has been prepared for them as they continue their journey.

Can prayer change things? Can prayer make things change? Would these things change without prayer? Would life be exactly the same without prayer?

No! Prayer is very powerful—the most powerful tool God has provided his people to make changes in their life.

God hears prayer, he listens to prayer, and he hears the pleas from the prayers. God knows what is necessary to change the course set in a life, God knows what is necessary to change the purpose or the drive or the notion of a life, and God knows where the change can impact life.

For instance, as you prayed to God to save your marriage and as you threw yourself on the floor and handed all to God, knowing that you were helpless to institute change that you had no control over—as you put your life in God's hands and put all your trust in God's hands—you had decided that only God could bring a change to a situation which you deemed hopeless. God felt all your fears, all your cares and all your love. He felt all your beliefs that only through God could your life be changed, and as God felt your power through prayer and as God felt your belief in him and his authority to change all that could not be changed on earth by human hands, did he decide to look at what could be changed in this plan of yours?

Did he choose to grant what you prayed for yet not grant the next what he prayed for? No. God is all fairness, all kindness, all sharing, all knowing, and all loving. He does not, choose to grant the prayers of one and not the prayers of another. Our Loving God does not do that. He answers all prayers, he answers all requests, and he answers all pleas, yet his people, his followers do not always recognize that their prayers have been answered, because they are not privy to what would have been without prayer. Only God can see this.

God responds and perfects what has been asked. God responds and perfects what is needed to keep each life on course, what is needed to bring reassurance that God is present and he is love, all encompassing love, and he will direct your life for you.

Dear Precious Lord, I heard Colton talking about how Satan tugs on one of his legs and you tug at the other and he finds himself in a constant struggle. Can you explain for me? Praise you, Lord, for loving me and for bringing me answers.

* * *

Beverley, you question the validity of Satan, you question your belief of Satan, and you question your understanding of Satan. Satan lives, Satan breathes, and Satan attacks. He attacks those he finds vulnerable, he attacks those he finds he is able to capture, those who know that their lives are in the hands of the world, in the hands of what motivates and generates the wants of the world, the lusts of the world, and the beliefs of the world, for the world now chooses to believe that money is their god, that success is their god, that ambition is their god, and they have forgotten that I exist, that I influence, that I can tempt. I can influence people to want to do good, to want to be good, and to want to encourage good. I can help people to know that love conquers all, love preserves all, and love protects all.

My people have forgotten to put me in their lives. They have forgotten to add me to their list of guests when they entertain. They have forgotten to invite me to supper. They have forgotten to take me along with them when they travel. They have forgotten to bring me the glory. I need to exist. Does that sound strong? Does that sound threatening? My power is influence through love, the energy of love, the energy of glory, the power of glory, and without this energy I cease to exist, the power of the world takes over, and this power is called Satan. He feeds off crimes, he feeds off hurt and abuse and neglect and dishonesty. He feeds off making the world an unhappy and unpleasant place to be.

Satan loves to bring the ruination of all that will fall into his trap, the trap of the world, the energy of the world, and the excitement of the world. Satan is alive and well and thriving off all the wants of the people, all the needs of the people. Needs and wants that don't include me, needs and wants that include selfishness, helplessness, self-centeredness, greediness—all that takes away from my love, from my peace, from my glory and my beliefs. Satan has been since the beginning of time, the energy of bad as I am the energy of the good. I need for my people to believe in me and to know that I bring the light of the world. I provide the light of the world. Without me there is no light, and without me there is no life, but without the belief and the love of my people I am not able to survive, I must receive the power generated by love, prayer, and belief, for all bring to the world the happiness of harmony, the belief that builds confidence, and the knowledge that I do exist, I do bring good, and I do know what will bring the world to a better place to be: the value that comes with human life, the purpose that comes with human life, and the creation of human life.

And so when Colton believes he is being tugged and lured by Satan, he is. He is being lured by the wants and desires of the world, yet he knows that I bring him peace, contentment, fulfillment, and satisfaction, and as this tug of war continues, rest assured I will win!

Dear Precious Lord,

Please explain the reason for homosexuals, and why, if God created them, they are condemned in the Bible?

* * *

Dear Barbara,

They are not condemned in the Bible. It just says that a man cannot lie with another man. It does not say that they should be stoned or murdered. Why is this so important to you?

God created every living creature. Did he create babies to grow up to be homosexuals? No, he did not. He did not create babies to grow up to be murderers, he did not create babies to grow up to be rapists, and he did not create babies to grow up and be grandfathers that sexually abuse their grandchildren.

God creates each soul with great care. He loves each of his children and only wants the best for them. God has also given us free will, and that sometimes can be a problem. Free will allows God's children to make their own decisions to choose light or darkness, and all of us have chosen darkness at some point in our life. Yes, Barb, even you have chosen darkness before. Many of us ultimately come back to the light, but most of our lessons are learned in the darkness—the darkness of deceit, the darkness of evil, the darkness of apathy, and the darkness of drawing away from our Lord and Savior.

Homosexuals make a choice to live with the same sex just as you make a choice to live with the other sex. Is one right and one wrong? Not necessarily, because it always comes back to love. God wants all his creatures to love one another regardless of their preference to their mate. God wants all his creatures to accept one another regardless of their living arrangements. Yes, Barb, this means to accept those people you feel revulsion for: the rapists, the pedophiles, the abusers, and the murderers. Can you do that? Not an easy request, but God wants his children to reach out to those in need, and the people you just named are in great need—need of the white light, the divine light.

So does it matter who we sleep with? No. It matters how we treat the people viewed as degenerates of this world. Extend your hand in love to all, even those you fear and are repulsed by, because we are all children of God, and the only way to show God's love is to extend our hand in mercy. Love all, Barb. It is what God wants of you.

Your Heavenly Father

Dear Lord, I continue to wonder about charting or scripting your life before entering earth. Could you please elaborate on this subject for me? Thank you, Lord, and praise you for all that comes from you and for all that returns to you. Amen.

* * *

Beverley, you question the purpose of scripting and the validity of charting the events of your life before beginning your life. Let me pose the same question to you. Would you consider not planning for a big event in your life? Would you just jump in willy-nilly and not even contemplate the errors, omissions, mistakes, and catastrophes that could take place? No, there is a need to strategically plan each step of every event to ensure success, to ensure low maintenance, and to ensure that it is perfected. As is your life, as is your purpose.

When you prepare to enter the earth plane, you must prepare for all events, you must plan for each event, and you must plan your learning. This earth plane was created by God to have a place for earthlings to come learn all that he wants them to learn. God knows the walk on earth is hard. He understands the struggles, but he also knows it is necessary for the growth and development of all whom he sends to earth. You have a choice, you know. You can choose to stay with God should you decide that the earth brings too many harsh realities, but only through your time on earth are you able to grow and belong to the kingdom of God.

God has many subjects who choose to avoid the pain and harshness of the world, who choose to avoid the realities of the world, but again, only through this adventure on earth are you able to understand what heaven holds.

Scripting or charting begins when your soul chooses to make a visit to earth. Your soul will choose the sex, the family, the hardships, the victories, the glories, and the failures. Your soul will choose the connections and the interactions, and the soul will choose the outcome. This is only a blueprint. The soul cannot predict the decisions of the brain once the soul is fully engaged in a body. The soul cannot choose once the soul is in the body, only work toward guiding, ensuring, pacifying, and soothing, and that's what gives you free will. Free will was given when the brain was engaged. Free will is what earthlings consider the brain and the freedom to think.

Free will can either allow the road to be less bumpy or can choose to hit every rut in the road. The brain has the capacity to overrule every decision made in the body, but in the event of overruling, the body loses its ability to become attuned or aligned.

But my question is still about scripting. I guess I wonder, does the soul script in every meeting of someone on the street, every action, every movement, and if so, how can you have free will? It becomes an oxymoron—is, but isn't? It just doesn't make sense.

But it does make sense. The soul does script every movement, every chance meeting, every connection, yet free will does exist! Free will is brought to the body through the thought pattern of the brain, *but* if the soul has scripted every thought pattern of the brain, then the soul has scripted the journey of the body and mind. When the soul is scripting, the soul is scripting for the whole being, for the whole body, for the whole person, and not just the events. The person becomes the event, and the event becomes the purpose. The purpose becomes the destiny, and the destiny becomes the life or the purpose of the life.

But I still don't understand. If the soul can plan this life right down to the smallest movement, then why live the life? What is there to gain? If it has all been planned, orchestrated to the last movement the growth could be in the planning. Is the purpose for the life on earth unnecessary then?

Not so! The planning, the scripting, the charting lays the groundwork. It lays the stones to prepare for the foundation, but it doesn't live the life, through coming to earth, through choosing to live this life, the soul now is placed in the body of resistance—resistance to the soul guiding, unless the soul has been able to attune itself with the body and mind. The soul grows wiser through each visit, each experience, and each adventure of life. The soul comes for the memory. Each life brings new memories for the soul, brings new meaning and purpose. The soul comes into the body as a flicker of energy but leaves the body as a whole. In other words, the soul grows with each experience, each encounter, each mistake, and each understanding until the soul fills the body completely through this growth, through this strength, and through this energy, the soul has been able to bring the lessons on earth with him as the soul soars to heaven. The transaction is very quick, the distance is very close, and the movement is unseen, for in God's world, souls are visible, but in the earth world, souls are invisible but for a very select few. Your Ryan is one who can see the souls.

A young boy who knows much but chooses to ignore all that is available in his attempt to protect himself from ridicule, looking to live in the earth world and not walk in God's world because he has not yet been able to bring the two worlds together.

Tell your sister to relax. Tell her to completely relax. Tell her to let go, because she still holds so tightly to her own illusions, and her illusions are not God's plans. She tries so hard to let go, but then they come right back to her. She knows that Ryan can't miss his calling, but has she ever considered that maybe he isn't meant to follow his calling until he is a very old man? Has she considered that her vision of her and Doug watching their son work with young children is a heavenly vision, one that will occur in heaven and not on earth? So, Barbara Jean, a precious child of God, put your fears aside, put your concerns to bed, and let this young man follow the script he wrote for himself.

Dear Lord, who are you and what are you? Praise you, Lord, and thank you for your love.

* * *

Dearest Beverley, I am. I am the wind that blows in your face, I am the sun that shines down on your face, I am the snow that blows up into your face, and I am the wind that blows your hair askew. I am the sun that beats down and bleaches your hair; I am the snow that pelts you with dampness, because I am!

I am the sun, the moon, the grass, the trees, the light of day, and the darkness of night; I am the warmth of summer and the cold of winter. I am!

I am the heart of the world, the love of the world, and the faith of the world, for I am!

I am all and I am nothing, I am life and I am death, I bring you the good of the world and allow the bad of the world, I trust, I believe, I know and I care for I am!

I am your God, for thou shall have no other gods before me. I am your God, for thou shall be obedient to me. I am your God, for thou shall believe in me. I am your God, and in this, you must have faith to know that my love belongs to the world, my love begins in the world, and my love is available for each and every creature I have created. It is available, it is plentiful, and it brings what no other can give, for no other has created you, no other has planned you, and no other takes responsibility for the lives of so many. I have the responsibility of ensuring that all have been given the lessons of life, the choices of life, and the decisions of life, and only I can give the purpose of life as you work toward what is the purpose of life. Then will you know the purpose of you and the purpose of me.

Search for this purpose, search for me in all that you do and in all that you have, and know that I am there. I am there to guide, I am there to lead, and I am there to believe that you can be all that you dream, all that you want, and all that you believe.

So believe in me and believe in you as you prepare for all that God has planned and for all that you have planned.

Dear Precious Lord,

My question today pertains to exit points. What is an exit point? How many do we have? How do they work, Lord?

* * *

Dear child,

A good question and one that has plagued you for a long time. The question of exit points, this is something that has intrigued you. Yes, my child. Of course, my child, of course, there are exit points, for how could my precious beings plan for their life if they were not allowed to leave when trials of life become too much?

Again, I remind you of the harsh realities of earth and the calming, glowing light of the other side, a light that constantly beckons those souls home. Again you wonder the why and how of the exit points, and again I remind you of the preordained points that are carefully sculpted to allow each and every one of my precious children the opportunity to return to their source.

When planning a visit to earth, we take care in ensuring that all is mapped out to allow for each being to be able to maneuver through life's hurdles, each jump requiring great fortitude and execution. You must remember that your visit to earth is much like a two-week vacation. You plan, you travel, you learn new things, and you continue to keep the memories alive by reliving the events of that trip. Much like that, in a visit to earth, you plan, you travel, and you learn and relive the events to keep the memories and the lessons from each lifetime alive.

As you move through that visit to earth, just like some vacations, you yearn to return home. Sometimes those yearnings become so strong you begin to believe the need to return is urgent and believe the only way to fulfill this need is through suicide.

Other times you may be perfectly content to lie back, relax, and enjoy the sunset. So are you the same about returning home—you are willing to sit back, relax, and wait for your exit point, and as the exit point approaches and you take a look around and like what you see, you may think "This trip is pretty good, and so I think I will stay for a while longer." And so it goes as you pass by one exit point and then wait for the next, then the next, and then the next. Exit points are very personal and very private for each individual as only they are aware of when they are, and as you question, "Well, of course, we don't know when they are," I am telling you that, yes, you do know when they are, and you do get to choose whether or not you are ready to return to your source.

As each soul chooses their exit points, it may vary vastly on when they choose to set these exit points. They may be years apart, they may be months apart or they may be days apart, that my dear child will depend on each soul and each life lesson they choose for that life.

Exit points are needed to allow each soul the opportunity to come home. Compare exit points to a highway that has exit points to depart from that road to return home. Think of that road and how many choices there are to find your way home, and so it is for exit points.

My child, my child, do not overthink or complicate the matter of exit points. It is so simple, so easy—they are just opportunities to return home.

You, my dear child, can choose whenever you want to return home by just choosing the nearest exit point, but let me remind you that the many lessons planned for each life are cut short when taking one of the first exit points, the only way to fully learn all that is available from this life is by waiting for your last exit point, and as each person struggles with the hardships and the frustrations with life, so must they appreciate the joy and accomplishments that also come with life, for with every hardship, there is joy; for every struggle, there is accomplishment.

Earth has so much to offer. Earth has so much to enjoy and to love and to feel. I encourage all souls to live their life to the fullest. I encourage all people of earth to look at the best in all, because it is there, and by finding the good, you are finding the joy. Life and earth are full of laughter and love. Embrace it until your last exit point, when you will return to my embrace and feel my love, for all my creatures return to me where they are able to bask in the everlasting love of heaven.

My dear Lord Jesus,

I have a question for you today, Lord. I would like you to explain to me about sin. Thank you, my Lord, thank you.

* * *

Dear Barbara,

Yes, Barbara, there is a lot said about sin! It is a sin to do this and a sin to do that. Where did the word *sin* come from? Well, Barbara, I will tell you where the word *sin* came from. Many, many years ago, before the time of Jesus's walk on earth, people wanted to control their counterparts.

Control seems to be the human's way of making themselves feels better. How do you control another person? You do that by making them feel inferior. You have seen it many times with your work with the women who would come and see you.

If you can make a spouse, child, relative, friend feel bad enough about themselves, it will give you the edge. It will allow you to make decisions because your counterpart will not have the confidence to make any decisions. It will allow you to tell your counterpart exactly how everything will work, because that counterpart has been beaten down so much that he or she will not have the confidence to stand up for themselves.

Now how does a good, upstanding citizen gain that power and control? How does that good, upstanding citizen ensure that the flow of life follows his needs and desires? Well, that good, upstanding citizen uses a different word, a different set of circumstances, and he will tell his counterparts that what they are doing is sin, what they are doing is not approved by God.

You see, my child, there are actions done by my children on earth that I do not approve of, but I am not the one calling them sin. All of my creations come back to me, each of my creations explains their actions to me, and then we talk about those actions. Do I give those actions a name that covers a multitude of different actions? *No!*

I do not lump together many actions under the title of sin. I meet with each and every one of my children separately, and we discuss their life from birth to death and talk about each one of their actions and why they did the things they did.

The word *sin* is used on planet Earth to produce guilt, remorse, and control. The word *sin* is used more in the language of God serving people so that it feels better when they go to their neighbor and call them on "their stuff."

Do not get me wrong, my children are not infallible, and daily they learn something new. They learn what guilt feels like themselves, they know when their conscience is telling them what is right and what is wrong, but most of my children do not need fellow human beings telling them they have sinned, because each of my children have me to talk to, they have me to discuss their actions with, they have me to let them know if they are following their path.

Ask anyone, anyone you like, if they know the difference between right and wrong, good or bad, light and dark? They will tell you that they know when they do wrong, they know when they do right, and they do not need someone else telling them they have sinned. They already know what they have done, and the majority of the time, they have already discussed it with me.

Does this mean that they automatically quit doing what they know to be wrong? Well, we all know the answer to that! How will we know what is good if we have not experienced bad? How will we know righteous if we have not seen evil? Life is about learning the good, the righteous, and we learn by experience.

Sin is inconsequential to me. What is important to me is that my children bring their fears to me, they bring their guilt to me, and they bring any action they feel bad about to me. Together we can solve any problem, together we can overcome any hardship, and together we will triumph. Triumph over bad, triumph over evil, triumph over sin.

Come to me, my children. Come to me with all your cares, come to me with all your sorrows, and come to me for comfort, because I am your rest, I am your peace, and I am your self-confidence. Come to me!

Your Loving God

Dear God

I need to talk to you, can I? I have some questions? When I die will my guardian angels still protect me or do I turn into one?

Love Bree

My dear Lord Jesus,

Bree would like to know about guardian angels and do they stay with us our entire life?

My dear Bree, thank you for wanting to talk with me, thank you my dear child for loving me and loving your fellow man.

Bree when you are old and it is your time to come back to me, back to your home in heaven your guardian angels will escort you here. You see Bree, your guardian angels are yours forever.

The minute you are born your guardian angels are with you and they stay with you until they have finished their job and escort you home.

When you come back to me and live in heaven you no longer need the help of guardian angels. Your guardian angels then can choose if they want to guard another little girl or boy or whether they want to stay in heaven and be close to you.

Bree, when you come back to your home in heaven you do not become a guardian angel, you will join your family that is already here and enjoy the most happiness you can imagine.

Bree, both Jessica and Jordina are very happy that you talk to them so much and listen to their advice. They will guide you for a very long time yet and you have two very smart guardian angels.

Your loving God

My dear Lord Jesus, thank you so much for your blessings, my Lord. Thank you for your letter to Bree. Now my Lord, Rhynn would like a letter from God also. Lord, Rhynn would like to know about babies and how they come after a man and woman get married. Thank you, Lord.

* * *

Ms. Rhynn,

My beautiful child—yes, Rhynn, you are my child also, I created you, my child. I decided the color of your eyes, the color of your hair, how tall you will be, and your personality. You see Rhynn, before I placed you in your mommy's belly you and I spent a lot of time together. We talked about your mommy and your daddy and your two big sisters. We talked about your school and what you might want to be when you grow up.

Rhynn, do you remember the promise I made you before you were placed in Mommy's tummy? I promised you that I would never leave you, that I would always be by your side, and if ever you should need assistance, I would be there for you.

The promise is still true, my beautiful child. I am always right beside you to help you in time of need.

Rhynn, I am so proud of you and the young lady you have become. I see you, Rhynn, when you take care of your cousin Hope in her time of need. I see how you treat your little cousins who are younger than you. I see how you treat your dog Deuce, and, Rhynn, it makes me happy that you are so kind to my other creations.

You see, Rhynn, all things on planet Earth are created by me—the sun, the clouds, the rain, trees, flowers, small animals, large animals, and all the children that one day grow into adults. So, Rhynn, my child, the answer to your question is that after having a long talk with the babies and deciding who will be their mommy and daddy, I place a very precious tiny, tiny baby in Mommy's tummy until they are big enough and strong enough to live in the world. I make babies and give them to their families.

Ms. Rhynn, thank you for your kindness to all my creations and being such a loving little girl. Remember, Rhynn, to spread that special love all around to your family also. Show your mom great love, show your dad great love, and show your two sisters great love. You are very good at showing love, so I know you will be very good at showing love to your family.

I love you, and I am proud of you.

Your Loving God

Dear Precious Lord,

Not long ago, an acquaintance was telling me about the death of a niece. When the parents went to a psychic, they were told she was in the waiting room of heaven because heaven was full. I have never heard this before, and of course, it has me curious. Does heaven become full?

* * *

My dear child, so curious, so quizzical, wondering, always wondering what happens when you cross over to the other side—always wondering, should you be scared, should you be joyful, should you be prepared to be left in the waiting room. Your life story isn't it, Beverley, always being left in the waiting room and everyone around you gets in before you. You certainly don't want to be left in the waiting room of heaven, watching everyone going in before you!

My dear, dear child, do not fear, do not fret about being left out in the waiting room. Heaven is full of wondrous rooms, rooms full of enlightenment, joy, fulfillment, and the love of God. All rooms are prepared to accept all of those choosing to return to their source. They make visits back to their creator prior to making their final journey. The soul has many opportunities to prepare where it will reside when returning to its source.

You must remember that the soul represents you in heaven. It is the soul that determines the whys, the how's, the when's, and the where's. It is the soul itself that determines if they will first wait in the outer chambers or if they will soar right through the gates of heaven into the arms of loved ones.

In a limited human body, it is very hard to comprehend the freedom and the full movement of the soul. When the soul begins its journey, it will stop at each room, each opportunity, and each venture to determine what best fits with their need for continued growth.

As we talk about different directions, different needs, and different purposes when a soul chooses to wait in the waiting room, it doesn't mean that heaven is full; it means they are still weighing their options.

Many times souls are planning to wait for their counterparts, their other sources, the other souls attached to their pod of souls to bring their whole back together, to regroup so to speak.

When there is talk of living more than one life at a time, of course, this is possible. Of course, souls belonging to the same pod are able to access more than one body in the same time period.

I know you are very curious about pods or groups of souls belonging to one another. It is true that groups of souls in heaven are the same as families on earth; they are connected. They plan together the needed lessons and then synchronize the lives to meet the needs and purposes of the pod of souls.

For example a pod of souls may decide that there is a need to learn the lesson of accepting assistance in everyday essential needs and incarnate into the body of a disabled. In that same earth span, they may also decide they need to live in a body that wants to share love with everyone or in the body of someone very selfish and is trying to learn the purpose of sharing and loving. This, my child, is the soul living more than one life on earthly time. It is just a matter of the one soul broken into pods to achieve great things simultaneously.

And so, should a soul choose to stay in the waiting room, it is more for the soul than the fact heaven is full. The waiting room is a great place to reconvene with the remainder of your pod.

You, my child, have nothing to worry about, nor does any soul returning to heaven as you prepare, and all prepare to return to their natural form. There is always room for everyone when knocking on the gates of heaven. Heaven is a very warm and welcoming place and encompasses all that pass through the gates.

Precious Lord, I have an important question I'm hoping you can explain. My question is, what is karma? I know that all things are possible through you, Precious Lord, and I thank you for all things.

* * *

My precious Beverley, this is Sarah, your spirit guide of intuition available to help you understand karma and how it works. Karma is part of what comes from God and returns to God. Karma brings the joys of the world to the people of God. Karma is available for all, and through karma, you feel God's love. He too wants this world to be free of pain and hardship, the evils of the world, and to know that love exists. Karma is love being transferred from one person to another, karma is caring for other human beings as God dictated, karma is available for all, just for the asking, for karma starts with God's love.

As God shares his love with you or any other human being, the love is so filling that you cannot store it all. You don't want to waste something so precious or valuable, so you pass it on. As you are passing on God's love in the form of good works, this also causes the energy surrounding you to change color as God's light shines through you.

You will be surprised at the color of God's love. It comes in bright golds and effervescence and shines so brightly. This light or energy is the power of the world. It is the energy that fuels our world and provides the light of the earth. The light will glow as the energy surrounds you. Karma is the name of this energy from God created from love that becomes overflowing.

Karma becomes the fuel that keeps our bodies from burning out. It becomes the strength that keeps us flowing and it is the love that fills us. Karma begins in one individual and is transferred from one to another to another until that piece of karma has burned out, but as that one piece is burning out, many more pieces are beginning, and the circuit of love continues.

As love comes in many forms, so does karma, and hence the reason good deeds are considered karma. Good deeds are always directed by love, and God is love. God's plan for the world is to share love, and in love comes the needs and wants to help those you care for, and although you might feel that you don't care for a stranger, yet you will do good things for a stranger. It is the overflowing love of God inside you that encourages you to help all.

How do you receive God's love? The same way you give love, you just expect it, and it comes. God loves all and gives to all. As they give his love away, so does he give more to you. The more you give away, the more you receive. If you are selfish with God's love and choose to keep it all for yourself, that love becomes stale from lack of movement and there is no opportunity to replenish this love because there is no room for new love and so the meaning of Karma—God's Love!

My dear Lord Jesus, thank you for all your gifts, all your blessings. Thank you, my Lord! Can you tell me why so very many people fear death and the way they will die? Thank you, my Lord, thank you.

* * *

Dear Barbara,

Yes, many of my creatures are fearful of death. They fear the unknown, they fear the unfathomable, but most of all, they fear leaving behind their loved ones here on the earth plane.

The people who fear death have no memory of their home here with me and believe their home is on the planet Earth with their families created on earth. They have forgotten there is another family waiting for them here in heaven. They cannot remember the beauty of their home here. They cannot remember the serenity, the peace, and the beauty of their home with me.

People fear death because of the unknown. What is ahead of me? Where do I go? Do I go anywhere? They fear the means of their death because, again, of the unknown. Will it hurt? Will it be embarrassing? (How funny is that? My creatures worried about being embarrassed after they have passed over to me.) They fear how it will affect their family and if it will be a long-lasting illness.

So, Barb, my creatures fear death because of the unknown and not having control over that part of their life. No control, funny isn't it? It is funny because no one—*no one*—has control over their life when they are alive. They think they do, but no one knows what tomorrow will bring or how they will deal with it. The unknown brings a loss of control, but in reality, our whole lives are the unknown.

If my creatures learn how to let go of control, they will soon lose their fears also—all their fears including death and the means of death. I would like all my creatures to know that there is nothing to fear—not on earth or in the heavens. I am beside each of my children and want only for them to put their trust in me.

Trust in the Lord, and all fears will disappear. Trust in the Lord, and each day will become a joy. Trust in the Lord and move forward in love.

Your Loving God

My dear Lord Jesus,

Why is it that so very many people have a fear of dying and the means of their death? Thank you, my Lord, thank you.

* * *

Dear Barbara,

There truly are multitudes of people who fear death. They fear the way they might lose their lives and are scared that it might be painful. Most of my children have forgotten the beauty of their home with me and are not sure there really is a heaven. My children do not remember that they were here in the realms of eternity where there is only joy, only serenity, and only that beautiful sense of peace and elation at the same time.

Anyone of my children can find a quiet spot and close their eyes and just sink into the place where all is calm, all is peaceful, and all is exactly as it should be. This is the place that my children can start to feel emotions here in heaven—the emotions of joy, great elation, and the sense that all is well, and never ever again will they have to worry about one single thing.

The fear is really not so much about dying as it is about "Am I worthy enough to enter the gates of heaven?" What my children have forgotten is that I created each and every one of them, and if I, the Creator, say that *all* my children are worthy of coming back to their Maker, then *all* children are worthy of spending eternity with me.

The fear of hell is not of my doing. I do not want any of my children to live in fear of anything. I want my children to rejoice in the fact that they are experiencing life on planet Earth, but know at all times that the short time they spend on earth is only a learning experience. Their home is with me, and that is true for each and every one of my creations. All come back to spend eternity with me.

I would never leave any one of my children to live the hard existence on planet Earth and then just leave them in the abyss. I want all my children to know, yes, there absolutely is life after death—life in an oasis of beauty, serenity, and a happiness only known here in heaven.

The manner of death has no importance because it is just a means of coming home. Very similar to how you and your husband always choose a different route to bring you to your earthly home, each human chooses a different means to bring them home to me.

The pain is not in the dying—the pain is in the fear of dying. Pain is always in fear, so when we can let go of the fear, the pain leaves with it. The most important thing for each and every human being to know is that I, the Lord God, created each one of my children; I, the Lord God, want each of my children here with me in *our* home. Let go of the fear and know that *you* will return to me, you will return to family already crossed over, and you will live eternity in happiness—a happiness known only by the ones here in heaven.

Let go of the fear, my children, because I absolutely guarantee you will be returning to me. I am not prepared to let even one of my children fall through the cracks. I will be there to catch you always. Let go of all fear and rejoice in lessons learned on earth, knowing that the eternal home holds only unconditional love and great elation.

Your Loving God

Amy, Lord? She has always been the glue that has held her family together, my Lord, and now she finds herself all alone.

My Lord, do you have words of comfort for Amy? Words to ease her pain, my Lord? Words that will make her journey here on earth just a little easier? Thank you, my Lord, thank you for your words of comfort and your words of wisdom. Thank you.

* * *

Dear Barbara,

Of course there are words of wisdom for those who listen to my words, those that follow my words, and for those that revere the words from their Lord and Master.

Your friend Amy is very lonely right now and feels like no one cares about her. Where are all the people that she has spent her life caring for? Where are all those people that Amy has helped many times? Why are they not here supporting her now?

Always her husband Greg was there to protect Amy. Always her husband Greg was there to defend Amy. Now what? Now who will defend Amy? Who will protect Amy? Who will be there if Amy is to get sick? Who will care for her when her time comes? All the questions Amy has been asking herself. What about me? When is it my time? When is it time for someone to care for me? Will it be her family? It does not appear that way. Will it be her friends? Well, there are not many friends left, and most friends do not take on that role. Who will take care of Amy?

* * *

Dear Amy,

My child, my child, I do know of your loneliness. My child, I sit beside you as you cry. I walk beside you as you shovel your driveway one more time. My child, I never leave your side. Extend your hand, and I am right beside you.

Your husband, you ask, how is he? Well, Amy, your husband is full of joy. He has never experienced the happiness on earth that he knows here in heaven. No one on earth can know the ultimate joy that is waiting for them when they return home to their Creator, and, Amy, you too will be reunited with your loved ones again. Many will be waiting in line to hug you when your time comes to join us here in eternity: your mother, your father, your sister, aunts, uncles, cousins, and friends, but first in line, pushing everyone else away to ensure he is first to welcome you, will be your loving husband. He too watches over you, my child, and it saddens him to see your tears but Greg knows that his time and your time are different.

You see, Amy, here in heaven it is but a blink of an eye, and you will be here, surrounded by all your loved ones. On earth it is different; the days are much longer, the pain is much greater, and sometimes it is harder to find joy. The long days and nights for you are but a mere second to us, and so our wait is but seconds.

Amy, my child, my love, what will you do with those long days? How will you find some happiness until you come back home? Well, Amy, I do not think it will come as a surprise to you that you are a helper. You are a giver, and I must tell you, you make me very proud of the way you have given of yourself. So how do you think helpers and givers find happiness? That is right, they help and they give.

You may think that there is no one to help anymore; you may think that you are tired of giving, but, my child, you would be wrong. There are many people in your community that would appreciate a helping hand from a woman who has always given so freely of herself.

Amy, that is how you discover your value, it is how you discover self-esteem and it is how you battle sadness and loneliness, by helping others. This is the perfect season to put your expertise into practice. You have been gifted with the ability to organize, the ability to listen, the ability to empathize, and, Amy, you have a huge heart—a huge heart with a huge hole in it right now. Start to mend that hole by extending all your abilities to those in need. Yes, Amy, it will break your heart when you discover what other people have lived through, but ironically, slowly it will mend the hole left in your heart by grief.

Do not worry one second about Greg and Shawna. They are happy and glad to be with me, their Creator. They are enjoying all the sights of heaven and getting reacquainted with loved ones, but they do want to see you go forth and be productive until you join them.

Your parents and husband are very proud of you and very thankful for the good care that you took of them and all you have done for your family. They want you to find happiness while you are on earth, and they too know that for you to be happy, you will need to give care and compassion to others.

Go forth, my child, and find a cause near and dear to your heart. Make that one small phone call that will be life changing. Take all those gifts I have bestowed on you and extend them to others in need. Again, my child, this is a good time of year to spread your love and empathy for all who are less fortunate than you.

Go forth, my child, knowing that in a blink of an eye you will be with your husband again as he too is excited to be with his wife.

You have much to offer, my child, very much. Go forth and share your love.

Your Loving God

My dear Lord Jesus, do you have a message for my friend Amber about her beautiful Jackson?

* * *

Dear Amber,

Your beautiful Jackson, your firstborn child, your son.

Amber, your beautiful little Jackson is happy and awaits the day he will be reunited with his mother. He plays, he runs, he jumps, and then he climbs into the arms of a waiting grandma to be rocked. There are many grandmas waiting their turn to rock your beautiful Jackson, and all have the capacity to love your son just as you do.

Jackson did not want to go through another surgery. It had only been three short months since he had been in heaven, and his memories were still very vivid of the ecstasy he felt when he was there. He didn't want the hardship of hospitals, surgeries, pain; he wanted to go back to his life in heaven, a life of pure joy.

Heaven's time is not the same as earth's time, so he knows it is but a few short days before he sees his mom again. He loves you dearly and occasionally stops his play to peek down on his little sisters. He smiles as he watches them in play and is happy for the family you have now.

Jackson does not want you to feel sorrow for him any longer. He wants you to know that he has a happiness that is only known to those who reside in heaven.

Jackson wants you only to feel joy when you think of him and to imagine the trumpets blaring the moment you are together again with your son.

Be happy, Amber, for the strong, healthy little boy that romps with the angels and the other children that chose the euphoria of heaven over the pain of earth. Rejoice—you and your son will hold each other again.

Your Loving God

My dear Lord Jesus, my friend Roxanne is feeling lost, Lord, not knowing what her purpose is, not knowing what she is supposed to do, and, Lord, how she misses her husband David. Lord, do you have a message of comfort for Roxanne? Thank you, Lord.

* * *

Dear Barbara,

There is a message of comfort for your friend Roxanne, a lady that has been part of the family for many years.

* * *

Dear Roxanne,

I know, my child, how much you miss your husband. I know of your lonely nights and sad days. Yes, Roxanne, I know of your sorrow and your sadness, and I want you to know that your husband never leaves your side. You are his true love, the beat of his heart, and his mission here in heaven with me is to guide you, Roxanne.

I know you want to feel his presence. I know you want to touch him, to curl up in bed next to him, and Roxanne, I am telling you that you can have all that. Close your eyes, my child, and smell your husband, reach out and touch his hand. Remember, my child, remember all the good times you had together. Look at the legacy you have made together, and when you need someone to talk to, just start telling your husband. As you drive in your car, tell your husband about your day. As you eat your supper, invite your husband to join you. Set a plate for him, grab his hand as you say the blessing, and know, my child, he never leaves your side. He is there to support you through all your trials, all your sorrows, and all your joys. No one need know who you are talking to in your car, no one need know that you ask your husband for supper, and no one need know who you curl up to at bedtime.

So, my child, let go of this deep loneliness and sadness and give it a try. Laugh at the thought that others may think you are loony. Your closest friends and family will understand completely.

Laughter makes the soul lighter. Laughter makes the heart sing. So find ways to bring laughter into your life. Remember when you could laugh at anything. Call back those times, and make an extra effort to laugh.

Your purpose you ask about, Roxanne? Well, child, what is your purpose? You have five grandchildren and more to come. Do you have a responsibility to them?

A grandmother is one of my greatest gifts, and of those greatest gifts, you are one of the greatest. Yes, Roxanne, you are a wonderful and devoted grandmother, and your five beautiful grandchildren adore you. You want more, you say? Well, Roxanne, you want more what? You want to be an influence in someone's life, you say? Well, how about the influence you have in the lives of five beautiful grandchildren? You teach them about love, you teach them about patience, you teach them about me, and you are the closing link to their sense of family, their roots.

You want more, you say? Well, whose lives do you want to influence? The homeless? No! The mentally challenged? No! The orphans? Well, no, you don't really want to deal with that kind of emotional pain.

Roxanne, you influence lives every day—your coworkers, your friends, your children, your grandchildren and your mom. If you think you still need to make more of an influence then volunteer. There are hundreds of places to choose from in the city you live in.

Go forward, my child, knowing that every single day you have an influence on each person you meet. I am very pleased to tell you that you have a good influence on the people you meet each day, but you can take it a step further. You can ask your coworkers "How is your day going?" and then listen when they tell you. Give them a hug, give them encouragement, and give them the lift they need so bad.

Influence your grandchildren by teaching them about your values, your morals, and your ethics. Influence your mom by asking her questions about her family, when she was a little girl, when she was a teenager. Does she remember how she felt when she met your dad, when she gave birth to her children? Let her life feel like it has meaning.

You see, Roxanne, you influence others with every word you say, every move you make, and when we are conscious of how totally influential we really are, we can change the world. I know you have heard it said many times, and it has become a cliché, but truer words were never spoken: "You can change the world one hug at a time."

Do you make a difference? Ask your children, ask your grandchildren, ask your mom, ask your brother, ask your friends, ask your coworkers. No, Roxanne, I mean ask them, take a survey—write it down, start with the words "Do I make a difference in your life? How do I make a difference in your life?" And then read the answers, find out what your significance is, find out what your purpose is. Yes, my child, you do make a difference. I love you and I am proud of you.

Now, my precious, precious child, go forward, knowing that you are capable of touching literally every human life you come in contact with. You have the ability to help every human heart move forward and beat with compassion and caring. I think that is a pretty big purpose. You are following your destiny as planned. Continue on soldier, knowing that both your husband and I never leave your side.

Your Lord and Savior,

God Almighty

My dear Lord Jesus, as you know my beautiful daughter-in-law is having a difficult time right now missing her mom. Lord, do you have a message for Katherine to make her Christmas a little more joyous? Thank you, my Lord, thank you.

* * *

Dear Barbara,

Yes, my child, there is a message for your daughter-in-law, but also for you, my child, because you too miss your mom. You too, Barbara, miss your best friend, the one who never said no to you, the one who never had an opinion on your activities, the one who was just always there for you when you needed a safe place.

Christmas is all about family, and you are now missing a big part of your family—the moms; your mom and Doug's mom—the ones you could not wait to go get and bring to your house, the ones who sat at the table and visited while you scurried around the kitchen. The moms, the heart of the family, and now the hearts are missing.

My child, your mother and mother-in-law both are with you as you prepare for Christmas. Both ladies are so very proud of you and how, even when they were here with you on planet Earth, you were the heart of the family, hosting the meal at your home, making sure both moms were well taken care of.

Barb, know that your mother and your mother-in-law flank you on each side, carrying you when you grow weary, cheering you on when you get depressed, and sending their love to you at all times. Barbara, you are never alone, and you have two beautiful ladies watching over you always.

* * *

Dear Katherine,

My child, my child, does life seem too hard right now? Does life seem too sad, my child? I want you to know that your mother never leaves your side, your mother supports you in all you do, and, Katherine, your mother is very proud of you. As you know, my child, your mother has a very important job to do for me here in heaven, and that is look after a very handsome young man named Logan. Oh Katherine, the fun these two have together, playing, reading, cuddling; all the time talking about their common bond—you, my child. You are the one who has brought these two together. You are the one who has made it possible for this reunion in heaven.

Never before has your mother-in-law written for you to help you understand why your beautiful son did not stay with you. Let me explain, Katherine, why Logan decided to come back to his eternal home. Your son remembered well the beauty of his home here with me, the tranquility of heaven, the peace of his heavenly home and the joy all feel when they are in the natural environment of their eternal home.

Logan did not feel he had the wherewithal to deal with all the struggles on earth, Logan did not want to deal with the sadness people feel on planet Earth, and Logan did not want to encounter the evil that exists on planet Earth.

Katherine, many, many of my creations change their mind about coming to earth as the time nears for their birth, because earth is a hard place to be. Katherine, not for a minute did Logan not want to be with the parents that he handpicked. He just did not want to deal with the hard, hard emotions and feelings that humans living here have to work through.

So what is your beautiful baby boy doing here in his real home, the home you will come to also? He is filled with joy—joy only known by those who are here with me. He is full of energy, and he is full of beauty. You will know him immediately when you come home to be with all of us here in heaven. You will know him immediately and understand better why he made the decision to continue living here in eternity where there is only great joy.

BEV & BARB MUNRO

Katherine, your mom followed her life plan. She knew before ever coming to earth she would be leaving early to care for her grandson. That plan was made before your mom was born and your son was born. Kindred spirits, your mom and your son, and they find great joy in each other.

Now tell me, Katherine, what other person could take better care of your precious son than the woman who was the greatest defender of her family? Katherine, your mom does not leave your side, she is always with you, and she brings your precious son with her. You can reach out and take your son's hand. Who cares what other people think of you? Talk to your, son. He hears you. Ask him his opinion and listen for his answer. You see, Katherine, you have a choice, just like everyone else on earth. Do you want to talk to your loved ones in heaven, laugh with them, include them in your activities, or do you want to be swallowed in sadness, not hearing when they try to communicate with you?

Put the sadness away, my child, because you will be reunited with your son and your mother again. It seems like such a long time since you lost both of them, but really, the time has gone by quickly and will continue to go by quickly. Enjoy your time here on earth with your husband and daughter. Each day is a blessing and teach that to your loved ones.

Enjoy your time here, Katherine, because before you know it, we will all be together again, and you will be guiding your daughter from this side.

It will be a glorious day when you join us, but for now, make every day on earth a glorious one for you first and then your husband and daughter.

Reach out for your mother and your son. They never leave your side. Reach out and feel their presence. All is well for you, Katherine. Enjoy your time on earth. Make each day a fabulous experience, knowing soon enough you will be with all of us again.

Enjoy your life, my child!

Your Loving God

My dear Lord Jesus, as you know, I am not confident about the letter writing right now, but it seems Sheldon could use some comfort in dealing with the loss of his beloved Melanie. Lord, do you have a message for Sheldon to bring him some solace? Thank you, my Lord! Thank you!

* * *

Dear Barbara,

There is a message for Sheldon today to help him move forward from his loss, but there is also a message for you, my child, a message to help you move forward also, and understanding that you have been given one of the greatest gifts ever. Do not doubt, my child, but believe in this gift of yours the same way you believe in your sister's gift—with all that you are, all that you will become, and all that the Lord has gifted you with. Believe, my child! Believe and glorify in this beautiful gift of being able to communicate with your Lord and Savior.

* * *

Dear Sheldon,

My child, my child, I feel your pain, I feel your sorrow, and, Sheldon, I feel your loneliness. I know that you think that I have abandoned you. You think that I have forgotten you, and, Sheldon, I know that you question my love for you. Know, my son, I stand right beside you. I watch as you work to make a commemoration of your beautiful wife. I hold you, my child, as you cry. I see as you curse me, and I hear your anguished cries of "Why?"

Sheldon, I would like to explain to you the whys that scream for an answer. Sheldon, your beautiful wife had a say in how her life would play out. She too has a chart that she follows, and her death was part of the chart. She chose her date of returning home to me before she was ever born, and your beautiful wife was loyal to the end. She honored her date of returning to her Creator even though she knew the pain it would cost her husband.

Let me assure you, Sheldon, you will be reunited with your wife again, and it will be for eternity this time. You see my son, time on earth is not the same as time in heaven, as each minute draws into a day for you, the opposite is true for Melanie. Each day is but a minute here in heaven, so it will be but a very short few days for your wife until you are reunited.

What will you do with your long, long days waiting to enter heaven? Well, my son, why not put this time you have left on earth to good use? Why not take this time to do things that you will be proud of when you stand beside me and review your life? Why not put those long days to good use doing things you will be proud of here on earth?

There are so many different ways of helping others in the small community you live in. Look around my son. What do you see? Who needs your assistance? Take this time you have left on planet Earth and make each minute count, knowing that Melanie is with you always, looking down with pride and love at the man she married.

Your wife is doing very well here with me, so you need not worry about her any longer. She is happy to be reunited with her family and knows that it is such a short time until you join her that she has no worries about that either.

Sheldon, your wife is always with you, so watch for the signs that your beloved Melanie is sending you. Know that they are her ways of saying that she will never leave you and she has not really left you.

Let go of the grief and be aware of her presence. Let go of the grief, knowing that in a very short time you will be with your wife again. Let go of the grief and take advantage of every minute you have left on earth to do something positive, something wonderful, and watch as your life changes and you give thanks for what you have instead of complaining about what you don't have.

You still have your wife, my son. She is right beside you. Talk to her as you drive your car. Tell her about your day as you eat supper and curl up in her spot when you go to bed tonight. She is there beside you through it all, and once you start acknowledging her, you too will hear her words in the quiet spot in your heart. You will feel her presence in your home, and you will know when she is with you.

Enjoy what you have, my son, knowing that you are still needed on earth. There is still work for you to complete. Be assured that when you have completed all that you agreed to before coming to earth, you will once again come to your home with me, knowing that your beautiful Melanie will be the first in line to greet you.

Go forward, my son, and finish the work you started! Go forward!

Your Loving God

Dear God, as you know, today is my dad's birthday and I miss him, could you please tell me where my dad is?

* * *

Yes, we can tell you where your dad is. This is Sadie, but you will hear from all three of us as you write your letter. This is very emotional for you as you cry for your dad and all the things you wanted to say to him—something so simple as "I love you," yet you weren't able to say that. What a torment for you to feel like you never took the opportunity to tell your father how much you loved him. But, Bev, he does know how much you loved him and cared for him. He knew this before he died, and he knows it now, he is always there for you, Bev, and he does feel your love for him. He also appreciates the love you carry for him.

This father you were afraid to say "I love you" to was also afraid to tell you how much he loved his girls. Truly his pride and joy, they brought him great pride in the physical world, and they continue to bring him great pride now. He wants you to know he appreciates you remembering his birthday and for taking the time to say happy birthday to him.

He is concerned about your mom and wants you to take great care of her, his true love and the woman who completely understood him. He knew his girls didn't understand him, but he knew they loved him with all their hearts and with all their souls. He very much wants you to pursue your plans to write letters for other people. He acknowledges that your soft heart was always your downfall, but it was your greatest gift.

He admires you for all the feeling you carry for other people. He wants you to know that your love for others makes him very proud and that he has stayed close to Shane as you asked of him. He wants you to know that your Shanie is a good boy, that he is very proud of this grandson, who has worked so hard to be a good father and to pay the price of his sins. He wants you to know that this son of yours, who resembles him, brings him great pride and swells his chest as he watches him work so hard on this house as he prepares it to be sold. He has been such a source of inspiration. He wants you to give him as much love as you can and to be there for this son of yours, who is so special. Your dad also wants you to know that all is well with him.

He has no more pain. Neither does he worry about money and work. Neither does he crave a drink. He is happy and protective of all of those whom he loves. He is suspended in a place that allows him to spend as much time as he desires with his family. He will stay here until his wife joins him, and then they will move forward together, very protective, ever watchful over your mother. She doesn't know he is there because she's not willing to feel his presence, but he is taking good care of her. Your father has big plans where he is. He is building and gardening in preparation of your mother's arrival.

Your mother is ready to join her husband, but her time is not here yet. She still has work to do. She is working on this, but you can relax. You will have your mother for a while yet, even though she thinks she is ready to go home.

Beverley, this is Sarah, and I would like to tell you about the place where your father is. It is close to you. Reach out your hand—that is where your father is. It is a place of joy and a place of glory and a place where all is well and there is no sadness. This is a place where people only want love and have no desire to hurt or maim or kill—a place of laughter and joy of heart. Yes, there is still the emotion that comes with heart, even though there is no heart. Where God is always present, his magnificence brings total love to all aspects of this happy place.

Believe that this place brings much happiness to all who visit as they prepare to return to the earth plane to be able to learn even more to share God's Word with all they come in contact with. It doesn't have to be in words, God's love is displayed by actions much stronger than in words. You will find a place overflowing with flowers, where the sun always shines and people as you know them are transformed to the image of God.

Don't be afraid of what we tell you, Bev. You are able to absorb all that is available for you. Take a deep breath and know that all is for you to share to help your friends. The people of the earth try to believe all that is there for them to grasp. Remember to be gentle, to be kind, to be loving, and to be soothing in all matters that dictate your response. Remember to put God in all you do.

At a place where, a square is cut away from a cliff, the cliffs are very high and does not allow for escape. It is a swimming area, with people around her. She is on a floatation device. It begins to rain, and she falls off her floatation device. As she is trying to get back on, she sees a shark coming toward her. She gets back on her floatation device, but the shark begins to bite at the device. This is when she wakes up.

Precious Lord, this is the dream that Joanne had last night. Would you please bring her a meaning to why she had this dream? Help her understand the purpose of this dream. Praise you, Lord, praise you for this answer to bring understanding for Joanne.

* * *

Beverley, you question the meaning of this dream, you question the purpose of this dream, you question the reasoning of this dream, and you question the value of this dream for your friend.

You question what message is hidden in this dream. You question what generated the dream and why it brings fear. It brings fear because your friend is full of fear. It brings fear because your friend is questioning her fear. A lady so confident, a lady so sure, a lady full of life and understanding, and she is now questioning why she would contain fear, why would she find herself fearful, what is it that is causing the fear, and how is she able to stop it, for she is not a lady who understands fear, nor does she believe in fear. She finds no room for fear in her life, but as of late, the body has taken on a fear of its own, leaving her to wonder, what has brought such a change to her life, what has brought such a change that she is not able to handle?

Her dream means much. It comes with much significance of all that she is feeling. She is feeling trapped by the high cliffs—the entrapment of her employment. She is able to signify the importance of having fun by the playing in the water and being surrounded by people, for her, people create fun and laughter, a good time. She tries to find the fun in her everyday activities, for she is truly a lady to enjoy the company of others.

As the rains come and as she is left alone in the water without the ability to climb up onto her floatation device, she is feeling alone, with no one to help her, no one around who cares to help her, no one around who has an invested interest in her—feeling all alone and unsupported, with no way to escape, no climbing to safety, no appearance of help, no activity to show her the way. As she finally climbs onto her floatation device, she realizes that she is capable of taking care of herself even if it is uncomfortable and cold as the rain falls on her, but it is only through her fear of the sharks—her fear of what would be without her job—that is she able to have the energy to once again climb upon this floatation device, her line to safety, and she hopes for security. She begins to panic with the first biting of this shark into her safety line, because she knows she has no hope of beating a shark, she has no hope of being able to escape a shark—to escape her position, to escape her responsibility, to escape her duty as she sees it. And as this shark continues to bite into her security, her feelings of hope—as her job continues to take bites out of her—she becomes panicky, she becomes very intimidated, which is not a feeling she is comfortable with. It is not a feeling that brings her any happiness.

Definitely the shark is the symbol of her job, constantly taking little nips, little nips until she is totally consumed with fear, the fear of having to stay, the fear of not having the courage to move forward, the fear that she will be stuck in this hellhole with no room for escape, with no means of escape, with no opportunities for escape. This is not a good feeling. This is not a healthy feeling, and as Joanne feels the pressure of her body, she questions again her motive for allowing such pressure to exist in her life.

Joanne, know your own strengths, know your abilities, know your own wants and hopes, know your own dreams for your life. Begin to live your dreams, begin to know your dreams, and begin to believe in your dreams. To know that dreams come from the soul, that dreams come from the heart of the body, that dreams are planted to bring messages,

messages for the body to understand, for the body to follow, for if you are able to follow your dreams, you are able to bring yourself the ability to move, the ability to bring movement, and the ability to believe that you are entitled to your wants and you are entitled to you hopes. It is so possible to make all your dreams a reality. It is so possible to make all your dreams come true if you will only believe in yourself, in the power of self, in the resilience of self, and in the belief of self to achieve, to be able to achieve in the name of your soul. You have so much to give, you have so much to share, and you have so much to bring to fruition as you again begin to question why you would allow yourself to be caught in such a situation, why you would allow yourself to remain in such a situation. You again question your own purpose for allowing this type of abuse, bringing you such strong feelings of fear.

You again question how you would allow such a thing to happen to you. You would never allow your son to stay in a place where this type of abuse was occurring, so why will you allow it for yourself?

You question the word *abuse*. You question why the word *abuse* would be used when you see it as tension in the workplace. It is abuse when you know you are being talked about. It is abuse when you are feeling unsupported and denied of what is yours, what comes with the position. You are feeling abuse, aren't you? You are feeling battered and knocked around. That is abuse.

So begin again to evaluate what is important to you—only to you. This is, today, about you. Begin to evaluate what would truly make you happy in this life, and then begin to move toward this, knowing you are supported, you are loved, and you are guided at home. Love is truly something that comes easily for you, and as you love your son and only want the very best for him, know that he too only wants the very best for you.

Dear Precious Lord,

Do you have a message for my dear, dear friend Cheri?

* * *

Dear Cheri,

We do have a message for you, our dear child. We have a message of hope—hope for your sister Elaine. Will Elaine get better? You ask. Not significantly better, but there is much to learn from your sister's illness as there is from any illness. This is an opportunity for your family to grow even closer, this family that has already suffered so much devastation. What does your sister need, Cheri? All she really needs is your love, your support, and your constant care. Barb does not want to write constant care, but we do not mean to live on her doorstep, we mean send prayers of love, telephone calls, little "I love you" gifts—all the things you do best, my child. All the things you do best, for you love the hunt of the perfect little gifts that say exactly what you want them to.

You are a very caring person, and each person you meet is the recipient of that care. You have the gift of making people feel good. They feel good just being in your presence, and you yourself can feel that attraction that people have for you. "So what about my husband?" you ask. "Why does my husband not feel better in my presence?" Well, Cheri, my dear, dear child, he does. He does feel better in your presence—you know that. It is why he always wants you to come with him. It is very sad that Cameron has spent so many years killing the love you have for him rather than building the love. Did Cameron do this on purpose? Oh, the destructive force of arrogance—the damage we have on people's lives when we think we are better than them!

Cameron's arrogance allowed him to think he could treat you as he liked and there would be no repercussions. There are always repercussions, always a price to pay for arrogance and abuse. Yes, Cheri, you were an abused woman, and we are so glad that you are now standing up for yourself. We love you dearly, and it pains us to see you treated in any manner but love and acceptance.

What to do now, just about thirty-five years of marriage? Is it easier to stay in the marriage, or should you leave? "How many will it affect if I leave? How many will it affect if I stay?"—Oh the quandaries. Nowhere, Cheri did we hear, "How will it affect me if I stay?"

"How will it affect me if I go?" It doesn't matter who it affects if you go but yourself. Close your eyes my child, and view life with your husband for another twenty-five years. Now move the movie reel to life as a single woman for twenty-five years. You choose. You choose how you want to spend the next twenty-five years, but, Cheri, just this one time, choose what you want. Choose what will benefit Cheri—not your sons, not your sister, not your husband, just you. Tough decision, but you are a tough gal, a good old farm girl, and there truly is not anything you cannot do. Choose for yourself. Choose what is best for you. We are always with you. Call on us for assistance, call on us with your problems, call on us when you are sad, and call on us just because. We love you, Cheri, and we want only for you to be happy.

Your loving God

Dear Precious Lord,

Please bring understanding and confirmations that will bring some closure to the events of this day—a day that has left Graham with feelings of failure, loneliness, and with questions unanswered. Any light you can shed on this issue is truly appreciated.

* * *

Precious Beverley, my precious Beverley, you care so much, you love so much, you are so much. You are caring, loving, and helpful, and you feel so deeply for all others and want to help all others come to me. I want you to know that you bring much to the world. You think you are just sitting at your desk at work and don't contribute to society. You think you are meant to do so much more for me, when in fact, you do so much for me. Give up your ego to love all. Find a way to protect yet to love, and you will find your lasting happiness.

Now I bring you the answer you ask. Why is it so hard for Graham to maintain steady employment? Why is it so hard for him to fit into society? The reason is because he is not of society. You wonder what it means when he says that he is not of the world or that he cannot be of the world but needs to be in the world if he is to work for me, and what he means is that the world surrounds him and overtakes him and leaves him drowning in the muck and mire of it. His sensitivity to this muck and mire is so much higher than those who are of the world. His sensitivity is so much more heightened than those of us who only exist of the world.

Unfortunately, Graham is among a smaller number of people who are in the world. I hear you, Bev, question, "What does in the world mean?" Well, let me tell you what it means: it means the world is his oyster to build and grow and bring the ripeness of God's Word to the people in the world.

This means that those in the world are able to change the face of the world by being able to bring joy, excitement, and love for the world of God.

Dearest Graham

God is mighty, God is holy, and God is one with us. He is the one to guide, inspire, and lead each of us to our final journey, a journey with many ups and downs, a journey with many disappointments, but also many happy moments.

Life has never meant to be a smooth road leading home. However, it also is not supposed to be continuously full of roads so littered with rocks and debris that you cannot maneuver through them, and so, I bring my message to you through the channeling of your friend.

Yes, I say channeling, as you are able to hear my voice through your head, she is able to hear my voice through her gift to channel.

My message is simple, my message is easy, and my message is clear. Get on with your life!

No more time spent moaning and groaning "Woe is me! I'm so picked on. I'm so called upon. I'm so leaned upon by those who don't understand me or what I stand for." Drop the "woe is me" attitude. It's not working for you anymore.

Instead, instead, my dear boy—such a son of God, so true to your beliefs, so true to your voice of God, so true to your ideologies—I say to you, lift yourself up, dust yourself off, and get busy doing my work.

Do you hear me, dear boy? My dear boy, so dear to my heart, so dear to the heart of many, dust yourself off, give yourself a shake, put yourself in the frame of mind to be able to complete my work.

Remember my message to you long ago. Do you remember me telling you in many different forms—through your friend's letter, through your own form of channeling, through opportunity offered to you again and again, through the ability to change the lives of others—do you remember? Do you remember me telling you over and over again, and then over and over again, and then over and over again to become involved with the youth of your hometown, to get involved and change lives, to get involved and save lives, to get involved and move lives—yours included.

Get involved in the movement of your life, a life meant to serve, meant to serve me—to serve me through volunteering, serve me through learning, serve me through love, and serve me through your desire and love to preach my Word.

Do what you need to do, do what you want to do, do what you have to do—choose me first, choose me only, choose me by honoring your desire to learn and love of the Word of God. Do this by making the necessary arrangements to fulfill your dream of spreading my Word. Do this by meeting your requirement to prepare for full-time schooling. Please do not waste your time with one foot in and one foot out of my world as you fiddle with trying to find ways to only partially prepare your training. Jump in with both feet, jump in with both arms, and jump in with your whole body to prepare yourself for the journey of a lifetime.

And Graham, never forget that I will never leave you or forsake you, but instead, I am always at your side, I am always at your calling, and I always, always, always hear your voice.

Rejoice in your love for me, rejoice in my love for you, and rejoice my dear, dear child, in the knowledge that love is the language of the universe. Exert your ability to love and spread this love everywhere you go.

Forget about yourself, forget about your hurt, forget about your anger, forget about your ego, and concentrate on me, the power and the glory of the world. Forget about what is behind and glory in what is ahead—my love, my dear boy. My love is ahead of you.

My dear Lord Jesus,

Do you have a message for my friend Bernice? Thank you, my Lord, thank you.

* * *

Dear Barbara,

Yes, there is a message for your friend Bernice, a friend who has always been available to help the elderly women in her life, the friend who only sees the best in people, and the friend who only wants the best for the people around her. Yes, there is a message for this friend, who waits patiently for her letter from God.

* * *

Dear Bernice,

My child, my child Bernice, you are my precious child, and yes, Bernice, I do hear your pleas to me. Bernice, I hear you as you weep for your relationship with your sister. You ask why—"Why is it I only have one sibling and we cannot get along?" "Does my sister even love me?" you ask.

Well, Bernice, let me tell you about your sister. As a matter of fact, your little sister does love you, and she respects you. Bernice, your little sister does not feel like she measures up in your eyes, and guess what? She does not measure up. Bernice, when do you say anything nice about your sister? Not often, not often at all! Why is that? Why is it that you do not say anything nice about your sister? Could it be that you too have feelings of envy? Do you envy Ginny's cute little body? Do you envy the relationships she has with men? Do you envy that Ginny has a new man in her life?

Tell me, Bernice, what does envy feel like? Does it feel sad? Does it feel mad? Does it feel discouraging? All of these feelings come rushing forth with envy and none of them are very nice. You see, Bernice, the only one envy hurts is you. When Ginny knows you envy her, it makes her feel superior. When you know Ginny envies something about you, then you get to be the powerful one.

You are very familiar with feelings of powerlessness as you have felt them many times, like most earthlings; you rather enjoy the feeling of power, but remember that power when put into the wrong hands or used in a detrimental way is never good.

Bernice, put away the envy you feel for your sister, put away the feelings of animosity that you have for your sister, and, Bernice, start telling people about all of Ginny's good features. You know them well, you know how much Ginny loves her family, you know what a good cook Ginny is, and you know she is a very good caretaker—that she put her heart and soul into taking good care of Morley.

Ginny has many good features. You only need to recognize them. You have lots of practice recognizing the good features of people around you; now use it to acknowledge all the wonderful features your sister possesses. Spread positive energy over this relationship with *your* sibling and watch as your relationship with your sister improves. Watch as your relationships with everyone improves. Love your little sister, Bernice, for if you don't, who will? Love your little sister.

I know you wanted this letter to be about Wayne, but your relationship with your sister is much more important than a relationship with a man you do not even know.

You have many wonderful surprises coming your way and 2015 will be a wonderful year for you, but I would like you to start the year off right by ensuring that your little sister knows how much you love her. How, you ask. Easy: little love notes, mail them to her; a text in the morning that says "Love you, little sis;" a small gift for no reason; some baking; a bottle of her favorite wine.

I can hear you protesting, Bernice, and I know this is the very last thing you want to do, but, Bernice, you are the big sister—you are the oldest, and you are the wisest. Small notes nothing grand; do not overwhelm yourself or your sister, but let her know that you are happy she is your little sister. I guarantee you; you will not regret reaching your hand out in love to the only person left on this planet with the same DNA as you.

All is well in your life, and your future brings you great happiness, so step out in courage, step out in love, and step out to give your only sister the support she so desperately needs right now. Step out, my child, and watch as all your hopes and dreams come to fruition.

Your Loving God

My dear Lord Jesus, thank you for your faithfulness, my Lord. Thank you for your blessings. Thank you, my Lord. Dear lord, do you have a message for my sister? Thank you!

* * *

Dear Barbara,

Of course, there is a message for your sister—a message of hope and understanding, a message for Bev to find more joy and that pot of gold at the end of the rainbow she is looking for, a message to move Bev forward as she approaches the years of advanced age and worries about her health grow even stronger.

* * *

Dear Beverley,

My child, my child, do you not trust me to care for you? Do you not trust me to ensure all is well in your life?

Beverley, my child, have I not always been right beside you to guide you on this journey called life? Have I not always been there beside you to give you the answers to your questions?

Beverley, my child, my beloved, I have not left you. I have not deserted you. I am still by your side. You can feel me. You can hear me. I whisper in your ear often, and you are one of the totally blessed individuals who hear my whispers. I will not leave you or desert you, but always walk beside you.

Trust my child; trust like your sister does. Trust that cancer will not affect your body. Trust that you have many years to spend with your family and that you will always be covered by my blessings. No, child, you do not have cancer. You will be fine, and once you truly believe that there is no cancer in your body, so too will the pain go away.

You have many years of learning this information. I encourage you to use it. You have guidance with you always. Ask them, and then listen to them. Has your guidance ever steered you wrong before? No; they are there to guide you, alleviate your fears and direct you in the paths to follow.

Trust, my child. Why would I give you this guidance if it were not to be followed? Trust that all is in place for you, trust that I want only the best for you, and trust that you have many more years on this planet to spread your wisdom. I would also like you to teach others about trust and believing. How can you teach what you do not do?

Move forward, my child, giving thanks each day for all you have been blessed with, and trust the guidance I have put in place for you. Trust, my child, and teach others to do the same.

Your Loving God

My dear Lord Jesus,

I come to you today to ask for a message for my dear friend Gwen, Lord. She is now right in the middle of one of the biggest crises of her life. Do you have a message for Gwen, Lord? Thank you, my Lord. Thank you, Lord.

* * *

Dear Barbara,

Yes, there is a message for Gwen and one for you, my child, the message for you is all is well, all is as it should be, and your future is like a shining star, so bright one has to close their eyes. You are on the right path, and I have been a part of everything that has happened in your life in the last six months. My child, I am right where you have asked me to be, in charge of the outcome and in charge of your future. Put the sadness away, because as you know, you have a fabulous life, and I will continue as I always have to guide you and bless you. Barbara, my child, your future is exciting and all that you could want it to be.

* * *

Dear Gwen,

My child, my child. Oh, Gwen, my precious, precious child, once again you are in the battle of your life, a battle for your life. My precious, precious child, there are people who do care about you, they care deeply for you, and you know who they are. Gwen, my child, I know you feel like there is no hope, but Gwen, always, always, always there is hope. It is what makes the world go round, hope. Without it, a person ends up exactly where you are now, hopeless.

How does that feel, hopeless? Even just the sound the word makes coming out of your mouth causes sadness. So, Gwen, *do not give up hope*! There is much for you to accomplish yet, and you will lose the opportunity to finish your life's work if you give up hope. This period you are going through right now is such a small piece of the puzzle that makes up your life.

As I see it, there are two roads for you to decide between right now, two roads that will take you to two very different destinations. Only one person gets to decide which road you are going to take. I know you have told your friends you are going to Safe Haven, but really Gwen—really? You are not sure about anything and definitely not going to Safe Haven, "a year in that—place, I would have to give up everything, even smoking." You say.

So now what? You know the final destination of both roads. You know what the journey will be like traveling down those roads. You get to decide. Only you, Gwen. Both roads very difficult, very difficult indeed. One road ends in life; the other, in death. Does that make it any easier for you, my child? You already know this information. You already know if you do not choose Safe Haven, your death is imminent, yet the decision is still a hard one for you.

The different roads also include different friends. The one road, true friends who care about you; the other road, the friends who need something from you and you need something from them. This is not a friendship, as you well know. This is survival, survival of the strongest. Are you the strongest? Yes, in your younger days, you sure were, but what about now? What about now, Gwen, as illness and age weaken you? You have seen what happens to the weak in the dog-eat-dog world you have spent so many years surviving in. What happens to the weak? They are used and abused and thrown away. Is that how you want to spend the last part of your life? Being used, being abused, and being thrown away? A tough way to live, a hard way to live, and a very sad way to live!

The other road will initially be just as hard to travel, but at the end of the road, Gwen, is reward, there is light, and most of all, there is hope— beautiful, beautiful hope. Remember the beginning of this letter where

I told you that it is hope that makes the world go round? Well, at the end of this road is what you need to make your world go around: hope.

So there you have it, my child. Nothing you did not know before, but now it is on paper as you requested. Now it is in black and white, and you can read it over and over again to help you make the right decision. Road 1 and the one you are leaning toward right now—death. Road 2 and the one you fear the most because it is more unknown—hope, life-giving hope.

My child, you have to make this important decision. I will not leave you regardless of the decision, nor will I judge you on the decision you make. I will continue to walk with you down the road of your choice, always by your side, always right next to you, but even with me by your side, your happiness is only guaranteed if you take road 2.

Well, my child, your friend has written for you as you requested of her. What will you do with this letter? What will you do with my words? You get to decide Gwen: finish your destiny, or cut it short? Choose carefully.

Your Loving God

Dearest Lord, my friend Pamela has a concern, a concern that she needs clarification to, an answer to put her mind at ease. Lord, I do not know the question or concern, but, Lord, you do. Can you bring her the answer or resolution she searches for? Praise you, Lord!

* * *

My dearest little Pamela, a child of God who works so very hard to bring resolution to her thoughts, who wants to bring resolution to all that leaves her with unease. My dear faithful child put your faith in the powers of the Lord to bring harmony and peacefulness into your life.

Allow the power of your Lord to bring you the solace and contentment that you search for. But you first must trust in your Heavenly Father to be able to bring you your dreams. You must trust in your Heavenly Father to bring you what you crave, and at this point in your life, you would still allow yourself to question God's authority over your own. At this point in your life, you are still feeling like you ask the question over and over and the one you worship should give you an answer, but listening as hard as you might, you hear nothing, you feel nothing, and you are no more the wiser for what you have brought to your Lord because you try too hard to hear my voice through your ears. But my precious little Pamela, my communication with you is not that direct; my communication with you is not that obvious. Oh, how you wish it was! Oh, how you wish it was that easy that God would just whisper in your ear the answers to all your fears, to just whisper in your ears his deep love for you so you could be assured of his protective love, yet you still question whether or not I even speak to you, because you hear nothing, you feel nothing, and continue to move forward believing that you are not answered. And so you will make all your own answers, unsupported, when in reality you are choosing to ignore my voice by being ignorant to my answers. They are there, my dear child. Each and every time you ask, I answer. Each and every time you have come to me in tears, in anger, in frustration, and in your love for me, I have answered you—oh yes, every single time.

Now, my beautiful child, let me explain how you can feel my voice, how you can understand my answers to you. For you, dearest child of God, you are a wise soul; you are an old soul, a trusted soul who has a very direct link with her master. A link she is not attuned to in this world, a link much envied by others, but because you always link yourself in the common category, you do not explore the options open to those who are not so common on this earth. You do not link yourself with those folks who are from a different realm, a realm I will explain as the heart realm for easiest understanding, a realm ruled and controlled by the emotions of the heart. Pamela, your heart is the ruler of your body and not your mind. Your heart is the dominant organ in your body and not your mind. It is your heart that makes the decisions in your life. You just don't believe or understand the dominance the heart takes. You assume it is all emotion and you will not be controlled or ruled by emotion and turn to your brain for your answers, and this, dearest child of God, is what causes your conflict with self. This is what causes you your fear and frustration in the constant battle between your heart and your head. Because of your strong earthly belief, the heart does not rule you, and you find yourself in constant turmoil in all events in your life.

I tell you now, child—and it is truly your choice to listen to me or not—my answers to you come to your heart and not your ears. My answers to you come to your heart and not your head. I will and do answer all your questions, I will and do hear all your prayers and bring comfort and solace to your heart, I will and do bring you the information you need to your heart, the living, pumping organ that is your primary life source, to where you will find all that you search for.

Trust your heart. Put all your trust in your heart, for you are governed by an active and loving heart that has held all my answers for a time when you are willing to believe in my answers, and know that the truth is there.

Your heart holds the keys to all you bring to me, which is much because you are a well-serving child of God who continually tries to hear my voice as she knows answers must come. Now, my child, I beg of you to listen to your heart, be guided only by heart. In doing this, you will be following my voice, you will be following the truth I have provided for you, and I will always be there to answer you.

Start to know my answers through your heart. Start to recognize my voice through your heart and know that you will never want for an answer again. You will hear my voice instantaneously when coming to me for an answer.

You will need to experiment in my answers to you. Ask your heart, yes, and wait to feel that emotion, ask your heart no, and then feel that emotion. Now try out other emotions, and see how the heart answers, and know that I answer all your questions and the answer is locked in your heart. Now unlock them.

My dear Lord Jesus, today I write for my friend Cassie and the struggles she has with her friend *Lois*. Lord, do you have a message for Cassie today? Thank you, Lord.

* * *

Dear Barbara,

Right now, your friend Cassie has many struggles, the least of them with Lois. Cassie struggles with confidence and how to move forward with her life. She struggles with the different men in her life and what boundaries she should put into place. Cassie struggles with the mean words of her daughters and the deliberate meanness of her ex-husband, but most of all, Cassie struggles with the relationship between herself and her mother. Is it no wonder Cassie is sick?

* * *

Dear Cassie,

My child, my love, so many struggles in your life, so many battles to win, so many hills to climb and swords to carry! Are you getting tired yet, my child? All those battles to win—oh my, that is hard work! What about all those hills to climb, not one but many? Are they making you tired? How about carrying those swords, helping others win their battles—are they getting heavy yet?

My child, are you sick, are you exhausted, or has the exhaustion made you sick? How many battles can you fight at one time, how many hills can you climb at one time, and how many of those heavy swords can you carry at one time? And then you put them all together, and it is now impossible for anyone to be successful.

So now you cannot climb even one hill, you cannot win one battle, and you cannot bear the weight of even one small sword. Why? Because you are trying to do everything at the same time instead of taking on each battle separately, climbing each hill independently, and, Cassie, for God's sake, put down the swords because it is not your job to carry even one of those teeny-weeny swords. They are not yours to carry.

All you have to do, my child, is to worry about what brings you joy today. Do not worry about tomorrow. It does not exist. Can you touch tomorrow, Cassie? Can you smell tomorrow, Cassie? Can you feel it? No, it does not exist, and yet you worry yourself sick about something that does not exist. Only today exists, so worry about today and find joy in the activities of today or do not continue. You do not have to continue working on something that does not get your heart beating a little faster. You do not have to be involved in anything that causes you resentment.

Now let's take a look at what causes you resentment in your life. Does dealing with friends who do not understand or get you cause you resentment? Does entertaining a parent who never showed you love cause you resentment? What about the men in your life—do you feel resentment toward any of them?

Let them go. Let the people that cause you resentment go! Of course, you may feel bad, but why? Why would you feel bad about letting go of the people who cause you stress and agitation?

Cassie, these are the reasons you are sick, trying to fix the problems of the world, trying to keep everyone else happy. When is Cassie happy, do you know what makes Cassie happy? Cassie, what is your favorite color, your favorite food, your favorite activity, your favorite song? Do you know? Do you want to find out? To do so, you need to spend time with yourself. Find out what your favorite activity is, find out what your favorite flower is. Find out who you are, my child, and then surround yourself with the things and people who make you happy.

Does Lois make you happy? Does Lois give you peace and joy?

These are questions you need to ask yourself, and then move forward, doing what is right for you—right for Cassie, right for your daughters. For when Cassie is happy, so are Emma and Jade.

Move forward, my child, removing resentment and negative energy from your life, and watch as your health returns, watch as your spark returns, and watch as you become filled with joy. Move forward in faith, knowing I am always beside you.

Your Loving God

Precious Lord, could you please answer a question for Lauren. She would like to know what her purpose is in this lifetime. Praise you, Lord, praise you for your love, the gifts that you present to all, and for the life that you breathe into all your creatures. Amen.

* * *

Dearest Beverley, this lady, Lauren, has been concerned about her purpose for a long time, something she spends much time considering and pondering, waiting for this answer from God. This lady finds herself drawn into her own concerns and worries, afraid that she might never unveil her purpose for this lifetime, afraid that as she ages and finds herself beginning to grow old that her life will pass her by, and with this life passing her by, so will her purpose. This beautiful lady, full of grace and full of love, needn't worry so, yet she does. She does worry about putting value into her life, assuring that God has such great plans for her and her purpose. She finds herself lamenting about this and finds herself anxious to find her purpose. Yes, it is a search for her, a search to determine her purpose and her soul, because she feels if she finds her purpose, she will then find her soul. Sometimes she feels soulless and that perhaps she is without a soul when she knows, in fact, she has a soul. She has a soul that feels the sorrow for others. She has a soul that rejoices at the happiness of others. She has a soul that knows what is right, what is wrong, what is good, and what is bad. She has a soul that leads her to the still waters, and she has a soul that lays her down beside the green pastures. She has a soul that sings to her, a soul that, when she feels down, will lift her, because she has a soul that walks with God.

She fears that all will be lost to her, fearing that her intent will be lost and that she will wander aimlessly, looking for her purpose instead of doing her purpose, yet her purpose sits in front of her, waiting for her to claim it. Her purpose is available to her any time if she chooses to claim it, but it is up to Lauren to claim her own purpose. Her intent was decided upon a very long time ago, before she was able to consider that she is able to be all that she can be, and this is what Lauren seems to be having her problem with—the being all that she can be—because she truly works very hard at being all that she can be yet sits and waits for her purpose. Lauren, is this not enough of a purpose? Is this not enough of doing God's work? What more could you possibly do for God than to be all that you can be?

Lauren, you are a special person. Did you know this about yourself? Did you know that you are made in the image of God and that, in this image, you are made to believe that you are loved by God, that you are loved by Jesus, and that, in all of this, both are well pleased with all that you accomplish in their names? You are the symbol they want representing them. You are what inspire others as you work to achieve kindness, love, understanding, and caring in all of those around you. What more could God ask of you? Well, in God's eyes, nothing. You are walking the path he planned for you. You are fulfilling your promise to your maker, and you are fulfilling your purpose. Yes, I know you ask, "Is that all? Is that all you want from me?" You feel this is so simple, so easy, just what everybody does, but that is not true. Not everybody does this. Not everybody can make a meal and invite everybody you know (practically), not everybody will help others with their gardening, not everybody uses just kindly words, not everybody just has kindly thoughts, and not everybody wants only the very best for everyone around them. You, Lauren, are special, you are a special creature created by God and tutored by God, and you are walking God's purpose for you. You are all that he could ask for. You are the reason so many people now worship and know our God, and then you still ask, "What is my purpose?" Well, God would like you to look around and see all the lives you have touched, all the lives that are feeling rewarded because of your touch. They are feeling valued because of your words, are feeling important because of your attention, and then you ask, "What's my purpose?"

Lauren, you have lived and you are living your purpose. You have worked hard for your God. You have served him well, and you have fulfilled your purpose. God is very well pleased with all you have accomplished. He feels your uncertainty. He knows you think you still have so much more to do in his name's sake, but God wants you to know that you are now free to enjoy your life. You are now free to do some of the things you have always wanted to do for yourself. You again question, "But what is my purpose, God? I just want to know my purpose."

Well, Lauren, your purpose is to love well, love life well, listen well, learn well, understand well, hear well, know well, and believe well, and these you now have fine-tuned to perfection. You, my dear, dear lady, are living your purpose. Pretty simple, you say? Well, maybe, but I don't think you still completely comprehend how well you are able to do all that you do for God. You take much for granted. You take much as just doing what you do instead of fully comprehending that this is God's purpose for you.

So be there, be available, continue to love, continue to believe, and continue to listen to God's voice, because he is always there, whispering to you all that he wants you to do. Remember, as you are living your purpose, that you will be led by God, and when God is ready to lead you to new changes in your life, he will gently take your hand and lead you to all that is available, to all that is for you, and you will then know all that God is ready to share with you. God still has great things ahead for you—not your purpose, for you live your purpose every day, but great things for you.

So remember, Lauren, that God is close, he knows all that you feel, and he knows all your wants and knows all that you bear and all that you carry and all that comes to you. He is always available to help, although you prefer to handle most on your own. God loves you, he is very proud of you, and he thanks you for your gentle hands, gentle voice, and gentle heart.

Know that God is close, and God is far. He is gentle, and he is not. He is here, and he is not. You will find him in the flowers you pick, in the grass where you walk, in the tree where the robin lives, in the house and outside. He is always with you, he never forsakes you, and God will lead you on all your journeys. He will walk beside you and take your hand so you will know you are not alone, he will walk behind you to protect you, and he will be above you to ensure that you too are filled with God's love and protection.

You have done well, Lauren. You live your life's purpose every second of every minute of every hour of every day. You have done well.

Now take the time to appreciate all this good. Take the credit for lives changed. Take the credit for all that you have accomplished in the name of God, because it is *great*!

My dear Lord Jesus, do you have a message for Esther as she struggles through once again another crisis in her life? Lord, Esther is trying hard to be the best mother possible, and she would appreciate encouragement from you. Thank you, my Lord, thank you.

* * *

Dear Barbara,

As you know there is always a message, a message of hope and encouragement, and these messages are meant to help people move forward with hope and love for all.

* * *

Dear Esther,

My child, my child, yes, it does seem that once again it is the end of the world, and Kelly will be the one to carry the shame for this event. My child, it is not as it appears. You have not yet got all the pieces of the puzzle. As you know, it is not over until it's over, and this mishap is a long way from being over.

There are many lessons learned from this event, many people will have life lessons from this event, and as you know very well, life lessons are not fun, nor are they easy, but yes, they are necessary. How would we move forward, how would we become all that we are meant to be without life lessons?

"Why me?" you ask. "Have I not had enough life lessons?" Well, Esther what do you think? Are you at the emotional level that you want to be at or do you have more life experiences to go through before you feel like "Yup I'm here. This is where my life was intended to take me." Do you think you are there yet? Not quite but you are making good strides.

Esther, how will you treat my people? Yes, Marilyn is one of my children. She too works hard to please me in a very difficult job. Cut her some slack. What about Chrissy? Is she not one of my children? Again, a child who works very hard, doing a very difficult job caring for my youth who have been treated so poorly. Both women are trying to make a difference on this very hard place to live called planet Earth. Esther, appreciate the difficulty of their jobs, and please realize both women are trying to help you and your children.

What about Corina? you ask. Well, what about Corina? Is she also not one of my children? Is she not also one of your children? Here is your chance, my child. Practice forgiveness, I know this is very hard for you, but I used the word practice because forgiveness is a process, and both mother and daughter have much to forgive.

Esther, do not allow Corina to walk all over you. That is not forgiveness. Do not allow Corina to use you. That is not forgiveness. Esther, what Corina needs to know is that she cannot manipulate you, she cannot use guilt to get what she wants, and you will not allow her to mistreat you, but you do still love her. Tell her that you will always love her, but love does not mean manipulation and guilt tactics.

Love means forgiveness, love means setting boundaries, and love means that I may not always be able to help you out. When the circumstances are right, the motive is right, and the heart is right, I will be there for you.

Your mom, you ask. Well, Esther, you are right. Your mom does not have much longer, and she too needs to feel like her life had meaning. She too needs to know that she had a purpose here on earth. Do not kid yourself, Esther, your mother is very aware of how she treated her children and granddaughters, especially her daughter Esther. Yes, she is proud of you, and yes, she does love you in her way. She is a woman with great pride and has not yet learned the power of an apology. Esther, you are teaching her many things, and now you will teach her the benefits of unconditional love.

Again, Esther, love is not allowing your mom to walk all over you. Love is not letting your mom say the hurtful things that are the norm for her. Esther, love is setting boundaries—boundaries for your mom, your kids, and your grandkids. You will teach them a healthier way to express love, a healthier way to receive love, and forgiveness is part of love.

This is a huge life lesson for Kelly, so do not feel bad for Kelly. He has chosen to learn many life lessons in this lifetime on earth.

He will grow into a man you will be very proud of, a man with a soft heart and a strong love for the underprivileged of this planet.

Never fear, my child. I am in the lives of your children and grandchildren. I am part of all that is Kelly and Delaine. I am in you, in Trisha, Faith, Corina, and your other grandchildren. I reside in each and every heart of the children I created, and I have a plan for each of my children, a plan to further them and prosper them.

Let go of your fears, my child, reach out for me, and know that I am always at your side. All is well, and all will end well.

Your Loving God

Precious Lord, I bring to you a question regarding my good friend Natalie. Can we identify her spirit guides to her? Please have my spirit guides answer. In all things I praise you, Lord. Amen.

* * *

Beverley, it is Sarah, available to answer your questions regarding your good friend Natalie. She too is protected and surrounded with spirit who guide and direct as she makes her way through each day. She has struggled with pain and hurt and must be soothed to bring alignment to her life. Natalie is well protected in her daily walk as she prepares to lead her life in a godly fashion. She too craves the love of God, but she is like a lost lamb stumbling in the wilderness, searching for her mother. She has felt empty and forgotten as she struggles in her search to find herself. Your friend Natalie longs for all that you have, not for the responsibility or the glory or the triumph, but only to feel the confidence you feel in your convictions. She too needs the love of God that is there for the offering. In all that Natalie does and all that Natalie says is the need to feel protected from the harsh realities of life. With all that Natalie has, she still feels forgotten and struggles to find a way to escape from these feelings. Natalie is guided by her spirit guide of intuition and by her spirit guide of emotion.

They are available for her to access simply by first believing and then by feeling their presence, not all is available for all. Just for Natalie to believe and feel that they are present to guide her will she be able to truly believe that she is worthy of God's love. Much has caused Natalie to lose faith in her God, for how could God love her if he wouldn't protect her from the harms she has been exposed to? That is the purpose of God, isn't it? To protect people? Yet God did not protect her from the abuses heaped on her. She too was left to her own devices to protect herself, and in all of this, what was left to hope for and what is left for her to believe in?

Nothing, a hopeless situation for Natalie to find herself in and to be alone with no one to talk to, no one caring, and no one to turn to, being left with so many feelings of guilt and shame. Where was everyone when she needed them? Why would Natalie believe that God would listen to her now when he didn't listen to her then?

Natalie yearns for the love of God but doesn't trust that she could ever rely on it. Natalie is caught in an abyss, swirling around and around with no opportunity to escape the continual thoughts of "Where was he?" "Why didn't he help?" "Why didn't he care?" when in fact, God never left her side. It is very hard for her to believe this when, in fact, she was still subjected to this torture, time and time again, blocking out the worst and only allowing herself to remember the parts least painful. Natalie believes that this robbed her of who she was meant to be, when in fact it did quite the opposite. Through all of this, Natalie learned the quiet skill of observing all her surroundings, preparing her for the hardships ahead. Natalie was given the gift of preservation, allowing her to be able to withstand the hardest knocks and remain standing. She too is able to call upon the support and guidance of her spirit guides and believe that Natalie is quite in tune with her protectors. She feels their presence and accesses her guides to support her through her trials and tribulations. Natalie's spirit guide of emotion plays a very big part in Natalie's life, lifting her through each and every day as she holds tight to all the emotion that runs like a current through her.

She still does not believe that she is intuitive, as she chooses to block her contact with her spirit guide of intuition. This scares Natalie too much for her to absorb, and although she blocks this guide, she allows access to this guide as she clearly sees the world before her. Natalie will find the contentment she seeks by becoming friendly with her spirit guides making jokes with them, talking to them out loud, and laughing with them over the funny things people do. As Natalie becomes familiar with these guides who direct in all that she does and all that she wants, she should ask them their names. As this relationship grows and she becomes more familiar with them, she should ask them their names and they will reveal all to her. As she becomes comfortable with her spirit guides, so will she become more comfortable with God and will find the courage to begin a relationship again to bring her the peace she so craves. For all things are possible through God allowing an opportunity to heal and find the strength to correct the wrongs made to her, the strength to find the courage to confront her abuser and truly explain to him the pain and shame he has caused but through her confession can the healing truly begin. For Natalie, all is well in her life, she enjoys good health, she enjoys prosperity and she enjoys the love that she feels when she opens up to the pain.

She feels cheated out of many years of happiness. Natalie is still afraid to admit that shame comes from blame of others, that healing only begins when the blame is placed back on the shoulders from where it first began, hard for Natalie when she finds it easier to carry the blame than to return it to whence it has come. She too deserves happiness without the weight she carries for another.

She will soon start to buckle over from all the heaviness and sadness that accompanies blame. All the should-haves and could-haves that cloud Natalie's brain are heavy-laden and bring no peace. Natalie is strong. She can carry the weight for a very long time, but why should she? It's not her weight to carry, it's not her responsibility and it's not her guilt. Why did it happen? In all things, there is a season. For Natalie, she too had a season of planting, a season of harvest, a season of barren and a season of growth. She is now in her season of growth to blossom and to come into herself. For this is her destiny to grow out of her pain, to grow out of her agony and to grow out of her fear and learn as she grows that in all things you will find God, in the blossom of the flower, in the ant scurrying past, in the trees of the forest and in her, for God did not forsake her, nor did he forget her but was by her side giving her the strength to endure, giving her the strength to believe that through all of this she was still worthy enough to live and she was still worthy enough to believe that she too was meant to find happiness. The search may seem long and the search might seem hard but what a rejoicing feeling to once again find God in her life.

You too Natalie are a child of God, made from his image, followed after the birth of Christ to be granted forgiveness in all things because in all things is God and God is in all things providing love and providing you with the opportunity to cleanse yourself of all wrongful doing.

Take God's love and take God's hand and let him lead you down the path that leads you to ultimate happiness. God too wants you to feel his warmth as the sun comes up in the morning, to feel his love as he wraps his arms around you, and to feel his presence as he surrounds you. God is everywhere, and he is nowhere. God is big, and he is small. God is rough, but he is smooth. In all things believe, but in most things put God for God is here and he is available to bring all the things you desire. For God has said, "Ask in my name, and all things are possible." Natalie, ask in his name, and all things are *possible*.

Precious Lord, I have a very important question for you. It is from a very good friend of Jeannie's. A friend she went to school with for so many years. You know her well too. Her name is Victoria Stetson, and she would like to know why the hell you would give her MS when you gave her the family she has?

* * *

Beverley, I will try to explain for Victoria the sequences of her lives. Victoria has also had many glamorous lives and has been many things in her many lives. Very hard for Victoria to believe—she doesn't even believe in heaven; how could she ever believe in reincarnation? But Victoria has chosen to return to the earth plane many times. She has been very beautiful women, very beautiful men. She has been very good, very bad, even evil, but do you know that in all of these lives, Victoria has never chosen to be sick?

She has always preferred to be strong, virile, and supportive. She has never before chosen to be helpless, and so as she considered this new life that she just began, it seemed her timing was here to put herself into a body that was helpless. Of course, for her now, it doesn't seem so pleasant, but Victoria too is only on this earth plane for a blink of an eye, and then it is over—the pain is gone, the humiliation is gone, the loneliness is gone, and gone is this family that has brought Victoria so many tears and so many fears that she too will be left homeless with nowhere to go. She has been under the pressure to locate a place closer to family, but "What family?" she asks.

What member would she choose to call family? None, not one of them. They are all selfish and self-caring, if it isn't important for one of them to remember her on her birthday, how could she ever corner them about looking after her? Who does she consider family? Jeannie. And, oh, what a sad life it is to live when the only person in your life happens to be a close friend from grade 4. Victoria has always wanted to be loved, even if it was just by her mother, but as her mother is too busy complaining to remember she has a daughter, when would she have time to love? What about her father? Well, that's right—what about her father, or does she have one? She had forgotten because it is pretty hard to remember somebody who disappeared before she could form a memory, jerk! Yeah, so it goes, the "woe is me" story for Victoria. Poor little Victoria, forgotten by God, never to be heard from again. The sad story that should have a book written about it: Poor young girl deserted by all but a kindly older lady who loved Victoria like her own daughter, just to discover her precious son had been doing things that weren't so nice. And what did this elderly lady do? Of course, sided with her son! Oh, she was still very nice to Victoria and still gave her attention, but she never made it right. She never made him realize that he had hurt her. How could she just let the whole thing drop if she loved Victoria? How could she do it?

Then to have her mom just play stupid because it was so much easier for her. She didn't need to make Victoria feel better if she didn't know that Victoria was hurting. She didn't have to confront Alex if she didn't know, did she? Very easy, very slick—just play stupid—something she did well back then, and something she still does well, doesn't she, Victoria? So much hurt heaped on one young girl, and why, why would God think that she could handle so much pain, so much torture? How does a young girl recover from all of this? Well, you know what, Victoria? You don't—you don't recover, but you do heal, and you do help, and then you heal some more, then you help some more, and I know you will ask, who did you help?

You helped so many people, and you help without, for one second, considering it helping. Victoria, God made sure you had one of the best personalities he could find to carry you through, and while this personality was carrying you through, it was also helping others. You are contagious. Once people are around you, they want to continue being around you because you lift them with your humor, your laughter, your ability to put a humorous slant on any story no matter how painful the story. Victoria, you lift them. You give them the gift of life, and that is

BEV & BARB MUNRO

laughter. You are an inspiration to people, Victoria. As you sit in your wheelchair, not able to feed yourself, not able to take yourself to the bathroom to clean and perform your rituals, what is left? Well, we will tell you what is left, and that is the amazing mind God gifted you with.

Such a brilliant student, never excelling to your full potential because you were also concerned with looking smarter, with being the quickest to get it done, being able to look not as smart but being able to keep friends. Sort of like with the Clarke sisters. You wanted to be their friend. You never understood why except even then you knew "I want them as my friends."

Victoria, you are capable of so much excitement just by living in your mind, to be able to replay each and every holiday with absolute clarity. You have yet to figure out that this is not a normal, average thing to do. You just assume that everyone can do that, when in fact hardly anyone can do that. Not only that but you have the ability to travel the world through your mind. You have been on so many trips that your life has been filled with adventure. This is not available for everyone, Victoria.

You too are able to retain the memories of your youth and able to go back in time and live your life all over again, replay it exactly like it was meant to be—another gift that you take for granted, when in fact that gift came right from God.

Should we address this MS thing, Victoria. I think we should, and then we will address this family thing. MS is a disease of the nervous system, as you are well aware. It does not allow you the freedom to live your life the way you choose, by working with the kids you love. And what else, Victoria? What else would you have done? Yeah, a little bit of travel, and yeah, you would go out with friends some, but mainly, it would allow you to go to school, come home, sit in the house, go to school again, come home sit in the house—but ah, with MS, what have you been able to do?

Visit Spain, a place you always wanted to go to. And you did, in your mind. Visit Scotland, another one of your favorite spots, and you got to go there in your mind. And what you like about visiting your places in your mind is that it is all your choice. You get to go with the most gorgeous men, you get to do the most exciting things, you get to meet the most extraordinary people with each trip. Then you can lock it in your mind and visit it over and over again. If you had not gotten MS, Victoria, you would never have had developed this gift. It would have lain dormant and undeveloped, as you know.

Yeah, we agree that probably this isn't enough for everyone out on the streets to be clamoring to see if MS is contagious and they can catch it from you. But relax and feel the love that surrounds you from all the people from a sleepy little town, and feel the presence of all of those you wouldn't communicate with if you hadn't got MS. Come on, Victoria, fess up. We know that you do have many gifts you're not willing to reveal, but you can tell Jeannie. She believes and she knows. She hasn't got the same gifts, but she has a son who does, so be honest. Give her the whole story It's time!

And so, Victoria, yes, you have the crippling disease of MS, you have the gift of bringing people great pleasure and giving them a boost to keep them energized for days, you have the ability to travel the world, and you have the ability to visit with people on their dimension. Do you want to give it all up to walk again? And then you get to decide and then you can go and talk to *him* about it. You know where to find him?

Okay, about your family—what about them? They are all morons. You really don't like any of them. It's just that it hurts your feelings to see that they haven't yet figured out who you are, and it would be a crying shame if you died before they knew, but you will, Victoria, because they do not have the depth to understand or appreciate, they are lost causes, and you are best to be able to do what you usually do. Let it fall to the ground, because the interest they have is all self-absorbed. As you already know, they'd be coming out of the woodworks if for one minute they thought you had any money. Little do they know!

So, Victoria, after saying all of this, why didn't you get one person in your life to love you? Well, because if you were loved and if you were spoiled, you would have missed the really good things out of life that God has given you, because you wouldn't have had the time or the desire to be the same person you have become sitting in your chair for hour after hour, observing, listening, hearing, seeing, and feeling. Be well assured, Victoria, that your next life will be much better as you already know, because you have it planned.

See you later. You know where to find me.

Love,

God

My dear Lord Jesus,

Thank you, Lord, thank you for all your blessings. Thank you, my Lord. Do you have a message for Stuart?

* * *

Dear Barbara,

Always there is a message. Always, my child, there is guidance, good advice for a young man who flounders, a young man that has not found his way.

* * *

Dear Stuart,

My child, my child, yes, my child, there is always guidance, always protection. You need only ask, my child, and you will receive. "Ask and thou shall receive."

Stuart, my son, there is a path for you as there is for everyone. Each of my creations has a path set before them prior to coming to earth. "Do we always follow our path?" you ask. Well, Stuart you know the answer to that. You know that you veered off the path that was meant for you. Yes, this happens often, but how do you get back on the path, you ask?

Well, my son, the answer is simple, very simple. Listen to your conscience. Listen to your conscience tell you what is the right thing to do. Yes, Stuart, you do have a conscience. Now listen to it. Do not plunge forward and do whatever you want, even knowing it is not the right thing.

When uncertain, Stuart, ask. Ask me the right thing to do, and guess what? I will answer. I am always with you. I never leave your side, so when in doubt, ask me. I may be a whisper in your ear, I may be an unexpected event that happens right before you, I may be the hammering of your heart or, Stuart, I could be that strong feeling in your gut that is screaming *no*! You have experienced all these signs of me with you, but you ignore them. Why? Because, Stuart, you want to do what you want to do. Look where that has got you!

Listen to me, my son, because I will never lead you astray, listen to me, my son, for I will teach you right from wrong. Listen to me, my son, because there is no one—*no one*—who loves you as much as I do. I created you, Stuart. I am the one who decided the color of your eyes, I am the one who determined your height, your IQ, your gentle personality, and, Stuart, I do not make mistakes. You are created exactly the way it was intended, so my son—my precious, cherished son—listen to my advice. Listen to the whisper in your ear, the hammering of the heart, and the screaming in your gut, and know, my son, I have given you all you need to become the man you want to be.

You ask about your daughter, your beautiful little Felicia? She is fine, Stuart. She too has a path to follow. She too must learn right from wrong. But you, Stuart, have the wonderful privilege of teaching her these rights from wrongs called morals. You will be honored, Stuart, to teach her about ethics and how to treat people.

You are a lucky man, Stuart, to have this opportunity to teach another from what you have learned, but Stuart, it does not have to be only your daughter. There are many in your community who can learn from your life experiences. Start small. It is okay to say to a coworker, "That is not right." It is okay to say to a family member, "What you are doing is not ethical," but remember Stuart, to preach morals and ethics, we must practice morals and ethics.

Show everyone around you that you are a good, upstanding, moral man and have the courage to call others on their morals and watch how your life will change. Before you know it, you are on the right path, and you won't even know how you got there. You have many years to put these new values into practice. Get started today, and it will change your life.

Stuart, you are very precious to me—very precious indeed, my son. I have never been disappointed in you—just patiently waiting for the time to come when you would become the man you were created to be.

Go forward, my son. Go forward and start the journey of touching many lives.

Your Loving God

My dear Lord Jesus,

I come to you today for a letter for my friend Jody, Lord. The past is coming back to haunt her, and she needs direction on how to handle this delicate situation. Thank you, my Lord, thank you.

* * *

Dear Barb,

First, a message for you my child, a message to help you with this sudden sadness and the sadness of your beloved cousin. You know well, Barbara, where Sandra and Larry are. You know that they have come home to me, their Creator, and they are enjoying great happiness. Family members met both Sandra and Larry, and both Sandra and Larry were overjoyed to get here. They are now experiencing all the wonders and joys of heaven. Your cousin Gail is a very strong lady and will be okay. Keep in contact often, Barb. Go visit, phone, send her cards—just let know how much you love her.

* * *

Dear Jody,

Jody, my child, my child. Yes, my child, the past does catch up to you. The past rears its ugly head, and each of us has a choice of how we want to deal with this dilemma of facing our past. Do we continue to bury all the emotions and feelings that come with looking at our past, or do we set out to make amends—amends to the people we have hurt, amends to our loved ones whose feelings were never considered? Amends are never easy, but oh, how much better we feel when we tell the people that are important to us that "I am sorry. I am sorry that I hurt you. I am sorry that I was so self-centered. I never realized how much I hurt you. I am sorry, and I want you to know that the ways I hurt you have lived in my soul for many years. I hope you can forgive me, but if that is not possible, once again, I want you to know that I am sorry for hurting you."

Who do you have to make amends to, you ask. Well Jody, who do you think needs an apology for the way you have treated them in the past? You are right. The list is much too long to remember everyone, but then, who are the people in your life who are most important to you? Who are the people whom you want to wrap your arms around and say "Forgive me. Forgive me, please. Please forgive me for the way I have hurt you."

Those are the ones, my child—those are the ones that need to hear the apology. Those are the ones that want to hear the apology, and those people, my dear child, are the ones that you need to make peace with.

Who will benefit from these amends? Your mom, your girls, your sisters, your brother, your trusted friends? Yes, of course, but who will benefit the most? You, Jody. You will have the most gain from the amends made to the people who are important to you. With each amends you make, a layer of hate is lifted from your soul. With each amends you make, a pound is lifted off your shoulders, and as you become lighter and let go of much hate that still resides in you, you can better go forward and do the right thing.

Step forward, my child, and do the right thing. Step forward and give credit where credit is due. Step forward and let your loved ones know that you truly are sorry for the hurts you have caused them in the past. Step forward, child, knowing that I am always at your side, and I would never forsake you—not now, not ever. I will be standing right beside you as you bare your soul and let all the people who matter most to you know that your intention was never to hurt them, but in your quest to just have fun they were hurt terribly.

Tell them you have changed and you are committed to a better way of life that you hope includes them.

Now is the time, my child. Step forward and go forth with love.

Your Loving God

Dear Precious Lord,

I don't need to go into the situation that Barb has found herself in to ask for your help, your guidance, and your instruction on how Barbara should go forward to find peace and purpose in her life.

Precious Lord, I again thank you and praise you for your messages of hope and healing.

* * *

Dear Barbara,

My dear Barbara, hear my voice. Listen to me. Bend your ear close to hear what I say, for I tell you over and over and over and over, and yet you then fill with the insecurities and the feeling of failure that envelope your body, and you are not able to put your faith in me to know that you are one of my protected ones, protected under the love you show on a daily basis to me and those who surround you.

I ask you again, would you rather be working and feeling completely controlled and molded into who you are not, or would you rather be free of such restraints to feel my love and share my love? In a position so dedicated by fear, anguish, and uncertainty, you are not able to bring the best to your position, much less yourself.

Let's go back to what you would tell a client. Let's think back to what you would tell your clients if they came to your office with the same story. You would tell them to love themselves first. You would tell them not to put themselves in a position that is tainted with fear and anguish each and every day they work. You would tell them to put their trust in God, that there is a rainbow at the end of the misery, and this rainbow waits for you too, child—a rainbow of brilliant colors and shades that makes you gasp with wonder.

The wonder of God's perfect world, the wonder of the perfection of life is that no rock is left unturned; no leaf is left to float to the ground alone. It is always supported by the wind to ensure a safe landing. As you are supported by your love and faith in God, you too will be supported to a safe landing.

If you are interested in the changes you are about to embark in, follow the same guidance you have given others, plan your visit to the chart room, and look at your chart to see what is ahead for you and then rejoice in all that you have and all that you are about to receive.

You are much needed in your community, so know that your services will be reinstated, where, when, by who, all for you to patiently wait to see. Again, put your arms up to the sky, feel my presence, and praise me for all you have and all you are about to receive.

Praise me for allowing change and initiating change that will bring you happiness and joy at all times. Feel my presence and my support through your last set of trials and tribulations. Give all of yourself, and you will receive all back. Feel all of yourself, and all will be felt back. Love all of yourself, and all will love back.

Be who you are, and know you are, my child, created in my image to love, love, love and give, give, give and feel the warmth and caring that this has for you.

You are a defender of rights, a soldier for justice, and a knight fighting for the rights of others. This battle is not just your battle, but a battle for a whole center. Why did I pick you to be my knight in shining armor? Because you are the only one strong enough, you are the only one with enough faith in justice to carry this off. My justice fighter never gives up, never gives in, and never gives away the power to make changes and to believe you are able to make the changes. Give yourself a pat on the shoulder and tell yourself "Good job" for standing tall in the face of adversity, for standing tall for the sake of others, for being willing to forfeit all for the love of the underdog. Good work, Barb, good work.

Your Loving God

Dear Precious Lord,

As I call on you and as I call on the souls of my parents and my grandparents, I feel their presence. I feel their energy, I feel their concern, and I feel their love as I bring this question to you, as I bring the reason for this letter to you in search of a healing, a healing for my sister as she waits in torment and pain, as she waits in the insecurity of her healing. Precious Lord, her message was to have her sister write for her. Precious Lord, I ask for assistance in channeling this very important answer for my sister. Precious Lord, please gift me with your message for my sister. Praise you and thank you for such great power and great success. Please humble me and help me with accepting all that you give in your name, Precious Lord.

* * *

My dear, dear child, such a devoted sister always willing to pick up the pen in defense of your sister, always willing to spare the time to bring her the understanding she craves. Dearest, dearest child, know that you too are well protected and well loved, that all your prayers are answered— your prayers that you may attend all your grandchildren's weddings, that you may be the greeter of all your family members, and that you will keep your health, your protection, and your love over all your children, grandchildren, siblings, nephews, nieces, and family members. I granted them in my name—granted in my name to protect, serve, and cherish all that is asked in my name.

I am happy to provide you with the necessary answers to bring peace and serenity. I am happy to bring your blessings of love, peace, and happiness, and I am happy to serve in the manner to supplement the requests of your heart, of your head, and of your soul. Believe in me, trust in me, and know me to bring you all that your heart requires.

Trust in me to be frank, honest, and truthful as I bring clarity and understanding to all things. Feel my presence, know my voice, and trust in my being to bring you your heart's desire, for all I want for you is to be happy. All I want for you is to keep your chin up, smile, and know you are under my protection. Know that you are under the umbrella of love, and so share all that I give to you freely, share all that I provide, and give freely all that you have; for in your giving, I am giving, and in my giving, you are giving; for in giving is love, and love is in giving.

Know I am always near to support, guide, and mentor you in all decisions. Know my voice to be able to discern your wants from my wants, for you know my voice, to understand your purpose, motives, and pursuits. For I will lead you into my wants, needs, and pursuits, but you will lead me into your wants, needs, and pursuits. Listen well, listen often, and listen intently for my voice, and all will prosper in my name.

Now a message for your sister—again a message for your sister to guide her on her road to recovery. A message for your sister to inform her also of her wants and needs.

Yes, Barbara, you do want your mother and father on earth with you, you do once again want to be that little girl who felt safe in the arms of her parents—both parents, nurturing, so loving, so patient, so kind, so sincere in their love. You want to return to this form of love, this form of security, this form of safety. You don't want or need the closeness of siblings, just parents who protected you from those harsh realities of life, protected you from all of that unfairness, from the cruelties and abuse heaped on so many.

You try so hard to protect yourself from the harsh realities of life, not what you experience, but what others experience. You are not worried or concerned for yourself; however, you carry such a heavy burden for others, and although you love your job, although you love the people you help, you also would love the opportunity to return to the loving arms of your parents, who protected you from the outside world by shielding you from abuse, neglect, poverty and apathy.

Oh, how you hate apathy! Oh, how you hate everything about apathy! You even hate the sound of the word because it sounds so weak to you. Apathy, what a word! What a stinking, stupid word that just fills the world with hate. For if you can't be passionate about something, then you can't love it. If you can't love it, then you can't fix it. If you can't fix it, then you must hate it. If you must hate it, then you must remove it. If you must remove it, then you no longer have it, and if you never had it, then it never was, and so it is apathy—it never was.

Never was what? Never was love, never was hate, never was real. It just never was, and so it goes for so many you counsel, never was: never was opportunity, never was pursuit, never was happiness. For how can happiness grow in such apathy? How can happiness grow in such hate? How can happiness grow in such a dismal, dark, depressive environment? Of course, it can't. It cannot grow in dark or in meanness or in ugliness or in apathy—it just cannot grow.

My dear child, you try so hard to leave all of that at the door of your office, and yet you just cannot—you cannot—leave all of those injustices at the door of your office, for you are a person of deep love, deep caring, deep feelings of wanting to heal, to help, to protect—protect all of those around you who live their lives in the depths of despair, who live their lives at the bottom of the barrel, scraping out a meager existence. And as you pray for each one of them, your soul cries out to me, "Help them, please! Please help them, Lord!" You cry in despair, you cry in pain, and you cry in anger that life is not fair. Why should these poor ladies suffer so much when the world has so much to offer? Why, why, Lord, must these women be deprived of everything: their health, their food, their shelter, and their dignity. I know you question if they are robbed of their food and shelter could I just sprinkle a little dignity on them—just a little, just enough to allow them to hold their heads up high; just enough dignity to allow them to walk out straight with their heads held high. Is that too much to ask, Precious Lord? Is that too much to ask of you?

Well, my dear child, yes, it is, it is too much to ask of me because you know that all is in my time, not yours. All is done in my time—in my time to eat well, sleep well, and walk tall. All is in my time to bring these beings of mine to a place in their lives to know they are loved and protected and guarded through my power and my love. These are all in my time.

What is needed for you to know is that success is not gauged by what you eat or where you sleep or how you walk. Success is gauged on what lessons are learned, what knowledge is gained, and what each experience brings to you in the way of forming your life path.

What you need to know, my dear child, is that you cannot heal them, for that is for them to do. You cannot change them. That is for them to do, and you cannot conform them, for that is also for them to figure out during this walk on earth.

But dear, dear child, you can comfort them when there is no one else to do that, you can encourage them when there is no one else to do it, and you can encourage them to move forward. But you cannot heal them, for that is their journey, not yours.

Your love is so overwhelming that it encompasses everything in your path, even yourself. Yes, dear Barbara, even for you, sometimes, your love is too overwhelming, and it would just be so much easier to revert to being a child, receiving all the love instead of giving all this love, for then you would be storing it instead of emptying it.

You must put yourself first over all things, all clients, all family, and all friends, put yourself with protection, guidance and love from the other side, call on all your family members, all your angels, all your guides, call on your protectors.

Develop a ritual to perform before all and any client meetings. Protect yourself from outside influences, believe in your ritual for healing and wonderment, and don't give so much of yourself. As much as you believe that you don't give so much of yourself, you give too much to remain healthy.

This illness you are now suffering with is caused by your strong concern for the injustices of this world. Your face is swollen and infected from all the internal screaming you have been doing about all atrocities committed on women: "Where is the equality? Where is the fairness? Where is the love for all these women left out in the cold?" Barbara, quit screaming. Quit this screeching out for others, because there is just one person you can change, and that is you. Take this week off and heal. Heal your pain for the unfairness of the world, heal your pain for the injustices of the world, and heal your pain for all the lost souls you want to lead to safety.

You cannot lead them to safety, Barbara. You can only give them a gentle nudge and then lean back and trust in your Lord to take their hand and lead them to safety. Trust your Lord to guide them in the direction of their lives and believe in God to know he knows what is best for all and he is there to protect all, to follow his master plan, in his master timetable to be able to live their master chart in their quest for growing and learning. Know that all come to earth to begin the eternal life; all come to earth to understand their eternal life; all come to earth under the tutelage and teaching of my words, my love, my protection; all come to earth to be placed in situations and locations that defy logic; but all are under my own hand.

So, Barbara, love—just not so deeply. Care—just not so affectionately. And protect—just not so protectively. Then you too will be able to heal yourself.

My dear, Precious Lord, do you have a message for my beautiful, caring friend?

* * *

Dear Grace,

We have a message of hope—hope for a true love, hope for a man that will attend to your needs, hope for a fairy-tale love story that all women want. Yes, Grace, there is another love in your future. Ask and you shall receive. Tell us what kind of man you want in your life, tell us of the personality of this man, tell us of the looks of this man, and tell us of the caring of this man, and we will bring him to you.

What about the last man in your life? What happened in that relationship? Well, Grace, you were just following the plan—the plan that was set out for you before you came to earth. Robert was part of your plan. He was meant to be the father of your two children. He too was following the plan. Betray the wife that doted on him, destroy a marriage of over thirty years? Yes, Grace, you did agree to all of this. I know—why the hell would you agree to something that hurt everyone so much? Well, Grace, when do you learn life lessons? When everything is running smoothly? What have you ever learned when the seas were calm? I will tell you: nothing. Nothing at all! We learn in hardship, we learn in turmoil, and we learn in sadness. You ask, "What the hell did I have to learn that I needed to go through all this pain?"

Your life lesson was unconditional love—love even when someone is hurting you, love even when being betrayed, and love, Grace, love when the hurt is so bad it feels like you are suffocating.

It is easy to love your kids, it is easy to love your grandkids, and it is easy to love your siblings. What about a cheating husband? Can you still love him? What about the monster that hurts the small children? Can you still love him? What if someone hurts your children? Would you love them?

No one comes to earth without a life plan, be that life plan long or short. No one suffers abuse without first agreeing to be abused. My children agree to abuse so they might learn and also to teach others.

Once again, Grace, you love very strongly. You love with great care and attention, but the ones you love must meet your conditions—the condition of being one of your children or the children of your children. Your conditions include the ones with the same blood running through their veins.

The hard part comes when we are to love the unlovable, to love the evil, and to love those that have hurt us. Again, a very difficult task. You did the right thing to divorce Robert, but you can still love him, not as a husband but as a human being.

The children? you ask. What about the children? Where am I? you ask. Where is a God who can allow this to happen to small children? These children also come to earth with a life plan, with lessons to learn, and to learn a lesson quickly and thoroughly, they may choose abuse.

Choose abuse? you say. I know you just cannot believe anyone would choose abuse, but each soul created by me does get to choose what their life lesson will be and agrees how they will learn their lessons.

I do not sanction abuse, I do not sanction betrayal, I do not sanction evil, but all of these atrocities exist in a world where there is free will, all of this exists in a world of learning, and all of these exist as the human race marches forward to a time of peace and love.

The goal for the human race is to break the cycle, not continue in the cycle. The goal for the human race is to rise above the hurt that has been inflicted on each of us. Rise above, Grace, the condemning of what you view as evil. Rise above the judging of men whose histories or life experiences you do not know. You do not know what they have suffered.

Your assignment is to let me decide the consequences of their actions. Let me decide, their Maker, why someone would hurt children. And let me decide what the world will learn from their behavior. Watch as your world begins to change. Watch as the evil slowly dissipates and the cycles are broken. This can only be done through love—unconditional love—for the man you think of as unlovable, and as the world starts to spread unconditional love for the unlovable, the earth will shift. The earth will see a time of love and acceptance, and the unlovable will become the lovable.

You are a part of the shift, Grace. Your love for the unlovable contributes to the energy of the whole planet Earth. A tough job you have chosen, but you can rise to the challenge and be part of the largest energy shift the planet Earth has ever seen.

Your future is bright. Your children and grandchildren are fine and will live healthy, long lives. Enjoy your life and love unconditionally.

Your Heavenly Father

Dear Precious Lord, do you have a message for my friend Rick, and if so, should the message be shared with him?

* * *

Dearest, dearest Beverley, there is always a message for all my children, children who come to this earth to learn all I have sent them to learn— children who come to this earth to be able to learn and grow in their faith, in their spirit, and in their love. As you know, for I have told you many times in many letters, love is the language of the universe, and without love, the world cannot exist. It is the fuel that keeps this earth ablaze.

Love—why do I choose to speak of love when you asked me for a message for your friend? And he is a dear friend to you, as you flood him with your love—love that he doesn't receive, nor does he know this love is available as he struggles to learn his lessons of this lifetime. Rick has been able to jump many hurdles in his fifty-one years, but he still has a few more to jump. Rick finds himself feeling alone and lonely since his father passed away. He has not been able to understand his purpose or his mission, yet he believes that he has a mission. Like so many others that have a mission, he would like to know what his mission is, when is he supposed to do it, why it has not been revealed to him, and why he has felt like all has been in vain if he doesn't discover his mission.

Rick, you do have a mission—a very important mission. You have the mission of understanding what happens around you. You ask, "A mission of understanding all that is around me?" You ask, "This is a mission?" You ask, "This is all you want me to do? Look at all that is around?" "There, it's done. I have looked at all that is around me" will be your pat answer. "See, I'm done. My mission is done. I have looked at all around me" will be your response, but Rick, nothing is ever that easy, is it?

No, I want you to look at everything around you. I want you to look at the trees that surround you. I want you to look at the leaves that lay on the ground. I want you to listen to the birds that chirp from the trees. I want you to see the clouds in the skies and notice the sun as it shines and the moon as it lights up the dark sky. Know that all has been made in my name, that all comes from me and all returns to me, and that in all of this, I made you—apart from the wonders of the earth, I also created the wonder of you. I created your strengths, and I created your weaknesses. I brought all that is good in your life, and I allowed all that has been bad in your life. I created the good to bring you all that makes you happy— your wife, your children, their spouses, and your grandson—but I also allowed all that brings you your growth of learning, the purpose of wise choices, the purpose of good choices, and the value of good choices.

Know, Rick, that all has not been easy, but from each that has not been easy, you have grown—you have grown as a man, and you have grown as one of God's children. Lessons are meant to encourage growth, and lessons are meant to institute change in your life. Only through change can we begin to right wrongs, make restitutions, and allow the body to relax into a state of rest and completeness.

Hard lessons, but lessons that were meant to be learned in this lifetime, Rick, you have jumped many of these hurdles. Let me help you jump the rest. Let me guide you to right decisions and right choices. Let me guide you to where you want to rest. You just haven't discovered this place of rest. I will lead you. You must remember to follow me. I will guide you. Now, you must remember to follow me.

As I guide you to this life you dream of, a life full of security, a life full of love, a life of family, and a life full of freedom. The freedom of choice, the freedom to choose, a life full of excitement as you watch your children and pray for them to have together everything you have had with your wife. A wife that has brought you much happiness, a wife who has brought you much love, you know that she is the only woman for you, that all you want from life at this point is to spend your life with this one woman that you love so deeply, so wholly. Rick, I have one request for your life. I want you to be able to talk to me. I want you to spend time alone every day with me—not a lot of time. You don't have to change all that is in place. I just want you to spend some time with me each day. It can be while you are driving to work, it can be when you are in the shower or watching TV, but I want you to start by saying "Hello, God. It's me, Rick" and start by saying that every day and pretty soon you will be able to say "Hello, God. It's me, Rick. How's my dad doing? Will you please say hello to him for me?" And I will reply, "Rick, you can say hello to him, for he stands beside you."

For this is what I want from you. I want you to come to me in your prayers and for you to know that I listen and that I answer prayer, and as you begin to pray and begin to ask me for what you need, you begin to believe that I am here and that I do answer prayer. Bring your wife into your prayer circle as you become more comfortable talking to me.

Rick, you do not need to share your prayer with anyone. You do not need to believe that any one will know—no one but I will hear your prayer. But for you, the gain and the reward will bring you to the place you crave to be.

Can you believe that my request is that simple? Can you believe that is all I ask of you? Just to pray? Well, it is Rick, it is that simple, just talk to me and listen for my answer. Notice it in the trees. Notice it in the grass, the snow, the leaves, the clouds, the sun, the moon, and all else that I provide for you to become this man I have destined you to be.

Rick, come to your friend when you feel the need for more written advice from me. What she gives you is truth. It is from me and it available for you. Just ask.

BEV & BARB MUNRO

My dear, dear Lord Jesus,

I thank you, my Lord, thank you for everything in my life. It all comes from you, my Lord, and I give great thanks. Today, my Lord, my sister and I come together to ask for your advice. Advice, Lord Jesus, on whether there is a need for us to do an internal cleansing, and if so, Lord, how do we go about doing this cleansing? Thank you, Lord, thank you.

* * *

Dear Barbara,

My child, my child, do you want to do an internal cleansing, or do you want to lose weight? There is a big difference, and the process is also very different. The process of internal cleansing is about going within and taking a look at all the resentments you still hold—resentments about your husband, resentments about your children, your siblings, your parents, your friends, your coworkers.

Each human carries resentment, and each human will benefit from letting go of their resentment. Do you have a resentment against me, my child. Are you mad at me that you got so very sick? Are you still mad at me that you are not back to your original self?

Well, yes, Barbara, you are mad at me. You try not to be. You know that many never recover and are in much worse shape than you are. Barbara, let go of your resentment toward me. I give you my word that your health will return completely.

What have you learned from this illness, my child? You say you don't know, but you do know. You have learned to ask others for help, you have learned to depend totally on another human being, and, my child, you have learned the true meaning of the blessing of good health. You never expected it to be you to get sick. You never expected it to be you that would be totally dependent on your husband. You always thought it would be the other way around. It is not you who smokes. It is not you who drinks coffee. It is not you who eats so much flour and sugar, so why was it you who got so terribly sick?

Yes, Barbara, you were terribly sick, even more than you realize, but, Barbara, it was you who had to learn the lesson of humility. You have asked many times to be humbled, but you are becoming fearful of how that might happen. You do not want to be flattened on your face. You do not want to be laid up sick for weeks. So how should you be humbled without such drastic measures? How about a little more time with me, my child? Some time to learn about humility from the Master, a time to let go of resentments, a time to give thanks, a time to just sit in silence with your Creator?

When should that time be, you ask? You know that if you set out time to be with me in the morning, it will be rushed because of all the exercise. After work, you are so tired. So when will it be time to spend with your Lord?

Is everything more important than spending time with me? You are right, Barbara, nothing is more important than spending time with me. Ten minutes in your quiet, quaint little office; as you finish your walk on the step for a few minutes; or when you get home from work? Spend ten minutes with me when you first get home and watch the weariness disappear.

Yes, Barbara, you are right. This is also a letter for your sister, and she too must find time to spend with her Lord. Is five minutes too much? No! Is ten minutes too much? No! What about fifteen minutes? Is that too much to spend with the one that has given you everything? For you and your sister, Barbara, spend a minimum of fifteen minutes with me every day, talking out your problems, sharing your sorrow, laughing with me in joy and giving thanks.

BEV & BARB MUNRO

Get into my Word, Barbara. I know you dread it, but push through. You and your sister can start together. Let her decide where to start, but read my Word, believe my Word.

As you start to spend more time with me, share your resentments, ask for help in letting these resentments go, and watch as the internal healing begins. Watch as the protective bulk is released. Watch as your midriff becomes smaller. But guess what, Barb? You won't even care anymore because you will have so many other things to talk about and share with me that you will hardly notice that the outer body is shrinking, letting go. And so now you know another way of implementing the saying "Let go and let God."

Spend time with me—you tell everyone else to do it, now why don't you try it? Practice what you preach, my child. Practice what you preach.

So now you know about internal cleansing, just turning it over to your God. Try it, my child. I am pretty sure you will like it. Write your letters as much as possible, but also please do not consider your letter writing as part of the "spending time with God" routine, for when you are in the process of writing a letter, you cannot feel the true beauty of my presence, the soft touch on your cheek, or the ruffle of your hair, the true joy of knowing you are in the presence of your Lord.

I know your struggle with church right now. I want for you to be happy, and right now, church does not make you happy. Spend the Sabbath with your grandchildren, with your daughter, something special with your husband or friends, and know that each minute you spend with these special people is because of me and give thanks.

I love you my child, I want to spend more time with you also. Go forward with patience and love and know that I have many great things in store for you, blessings in great abundance. I love you dearly.

Lord God

Xoxoxo

My dear Lord Jesus,

Do you have a message for Summer on the delicate matter of talking to her friend?

Thank you, my Lord, thank you.

* * *

Dear Barbara,

As you know, my child, there is always a message to bring peace, to bring hope, to bring advice to those who take the advice. Your friend Summer is one of the few who take the message I give them and then live their life according to the message.

* * *

Dear Summer,

Advice on how to broach a delicate subject with your friend—a friend that you love dearly and only wants the best for. Summer, you already know the answer to this question. Of course you talk to your dear friend Brit about her behavior. Of course you tell her that her behavior is not indicative of whom she truly is.

You see, Summer, your dear friend Brit is a true child of mine. Brit has always known me, always loved me, and always come to me for advice. Brit does not always take my advice, as you have observed yourself, but please know that my beautiful Brit loves me with all her heart and soul.

Brit is in a phase of her life where she does not want to listen to me. She is angry with me right now. Can you tell? Brit is angry because she thinks I should have stopped the marriage to Andrew before she gave him twenty years of her life. Twenty wasted years is Brit's thought, but never is a second on earth wasted time—not even a second.

Brit is trying to prove to me that she can go back and she can undo what she thinks I put together. She is not happy right now, as much as she tries to show everyone in her life that she is. Brit is trying to play catch-up on her teen years—a very difficult thing to do in your forties—but Brit will discover what she is looking for, and may be surprised to discover it is not a man who will make her happy. Brit can only find happiness when she looks for it within herself. She will find happiness when she once again brings her trials and her burden to her Lord and Savior.

Summer, how do you help this friend you love so much? Exactly the way you are treating her now, with love and nonjudgment. Summer, you are the very best at unconditional love, and that is what your friend needs right now. Someone who loves her regardless of how she acts, someone who loves her regardless of what she says, someone who loves her regardless of how often she can return that same level of love.

Summer, that friend is you—you are the one who can give Brit unconditional love. Summer, I am going to make this very easy for you because Brit is going to get her own letter. Take Brit for lunch. Pick up some little gift and then give her this beautiful gift of a letter from God.

Thank you for being the kind of friend every girl wants. Thank you, Summer.

* * *

Dear Brit,

My child, my child, my beautiful precious child! I want you to know that I love you very much. Brit, it does not matter what you do, it does not matter what you say, it does not matter how often you yell at me, swear at me, threaten me, I love you!

I love you regardless of your actions. I love you regardless of your words. Brit, you are my child, my child, created by me. I will never ever give up on you! Do not think I will love you more when you are sitting in a pew in church. Do not think I will love you more when your nose is burrowed in the Bible. Do not think I will love you more when you are spreading the Gospel, because, Brit, I love you the same—good or bad, it makes no difference to me.

Brit, I will never leave your side. No matter the circumstance, I am beside you. I love you, my child, regardless of your actions, regardless of your words, and regardless of your thoughts, because you see, my child, I know you. I know Brit! I know your heart, I know your compassion, and I know your caring. Nothing will make me love you less. Nothing.

So my precious, dear child, it does not matter how much you try to push me away. It will not work. No matter how much you think I may be angry with you, you would be wrong. I will never be angry with you. That is not what I do—that is a human thing. No matter how much you curse me, I will not get angry with you. You see, my beautiful child, I am here to love you, not judge you. Again, judging is not my thing but a human thing. I am here to give you absolute, unconditional love. I am here to walk beside you as you learn the lessons of life. I am here to give you advice when you seek it out, and, my beautiful child, I am here to support you through all your trials.

I am not going to condemn you to hell, I am not going to judge you, and I am not going to interfere with the decisions you make. *But* I am here to turn to when you are sad and lonely. Talk to me. I am here when you allow feelings of guilt to overtake your body. Reach out for me. I am here as you fill with doubt and indecisiveness. Ask my opinion.

Brit, I never leave your side, and I am here beside you to encourage you, to fill you with hope, and for you to feel my love envelop you from head to toe. Now, my child put away your fears. Do not think I am angry with you. I am not. Do not think I am judging you. I am not. Do not think I have quit loving you. That will never happen.

Before you came to earth, I made you a promise when you were still in heaven, and that promise was that I will never leave you and I will never forsake you, and my child, I never ever go back on my promises.

Brit, I want you to move forward, not worrying about what I think of you because I think you are awesome. I want you to move forward, not worrying about whether I am mad at you. I do not get mad at my children. I want you to move forward knowing that I do not judge you. I am here to support you and love you.

This is what I want from you, my child, a few minutes of your time each day conversing with me. Just a few minutes to start with. In your car, in your office, in your bedroom—the location does not matter, just a few minutes to tell me your concerns, to tell me your troubles, to tell me your thoughts. Just some alone time for you and me, my child, some time for you to feel my love, feel my strength, and feel my encouragement.

Brit, go forward knowing that it matters not what you do, what you say, or what you think. I will love you forever and ever. Go forward, and enjoy this life you so carefully chose before coming to earth. Yes, my child, you chose, so go forward loving every minute of your time on earth, because soon enough, you will come back to me, my child, and you will not want to have any regrets for your time spent on earth.

Go forward, Brit, knowing I never leave your side, I do not judge, and you are all I created you to be. Go forward, my child.

Your Loving God

Dear Precious Lord,

Please hear my call for help. Lord, please hear my cry as I feel completely forgotten, I feel completely betrayed, I feel all alone, which is not a good feeling for someone who has been married for forty years.

* * *

My dear little child, all curled up in ball, crying your heart out all your life. You just wanted to be shown some attention. Your whole life you just wanted to feel loved, and yet you don't feel anyone has or does love you.

You give everything you have to those around you just to get a little love back, and yet you don't even feel loved a little bit. You feel ignored by everyone around you. You feel rejected and betrayed by everyone around you. The thing you have always wanted the most in your life eludes you, out of your grasp, and you are just too tired to even try anymore.

Even the ones you tried the hardest to have love you have no time for you, growing up before your eyes, busy with everything else but with no time for their grandma. What a sad state of affairs for our little Beverley, feeling completely unloved, unappreciated, and undeserving of all the love she gives out so freely just to get a little love back.

My dear little child, my precious little child, so many years spent loving others and always forgetting to love yourself, always forgetting to put yourself first.

What can we do to help you when you still get all your personal love through things, through wanting things. How can we teach you to love yourself when you put all your love into possessions because you just don't know how to give yourself love, when you're so busy trying to get love from others that you forget the number one rule, love yourself first.

Love yourself as the person most important to you. Who is that person? Who is that person that is most important to you? It needs to be you. It has to be you to find internal happiness, for external happiness is false. It is found in fake things that are not consistent, that are not fulfilling, that are not obtainable. But internal love is always available for you to capture.

How do you self-love? How do you feel self-love? By giving it, embracing it, feeling it, living it. Start again by imagining yourself on a deserted island with just yourself. Start again by having your own conversation about loving you.

You so want external love, but for now, let's focus on internal love. Let's focus on turning all of that outward love inward. Let's start by taking that huge abundance of love you have for the outside and turning it inward.

How do you do that?

How do you do that, dear child? How do you learn to love yourself well? Of course, by telling yourself that you love you! Say it with affection, truth, and meaning. Say it all the time, repeating it over and over and over and over. Believe it truly. Believe that you love yourself.

Precious Lord, a friend of Barb's has a question for you. Could you please have my spirit guides answer for her? Her question is, "Dear God, I have never felt you in my life. Show me that you are here, and why doesn't my mom love me. I'm forty-seven years old, and I feel like I have never had anything."

* * *

Dearest Beverley, this is your spirit guide Sarah. This message is for Danni from God. Danni, as all of God's children are well loved and protected, you are also. You are protected by the love that God gives, and you are protected by his earthly protectors. You have protection all around you. You have spirit guides to guide you, and they do guide. You just don't recognize their voices. They surround you. One is on your left, and if you talk to her, she will answer her name is Martha, very close, always advising, suggesting, even lecturing. On the right, you are protected by three spirit guides. The first, close to your ear, is your spirit guide of emotions, available to guide you through your lows, to lift you from depression, to allow you the rejoicing you can feel at times. Your spirit guide of emotion is called Samuel, always listening, always supporting, and always there as you feel yourself falling, falling into depression, or lows as I like to call them. Call out to Samuel, tell him how you feel, and ask him to lift you out of this low, as you really don't like being there. You also have two more spirit guides, and you are very well protected. Your other two spirit guides are from the spirit world. One is a little closer to you, as you hear him singing to you. Your fourth spirit guide is even farther away, always watching, always guiding, and always available as you begin the journey of happiness in preparing for the new Danni to emerge and find all that she has dreamed of. She has dreamed of the fruit on the trees. She has dreamed of the flowers popping up from the ground to signify a new beginning, and she has dreamed of falling in love with a man—a tall man with brown hair, a brown mustache, and soft brown eyes. A man who is gentle. A man who is loving. A man who is kind and a man who loves you.

A recurring dream that just never seems to come to fruition; hence, the fruits on the trees. Danni, believe that you too deserve happiness, you deserve love, and you deserve to be loved by God. You are a woman who has experienced many hardships, many tumultuous relationships. If God truly loves you, why would he subject you to this kind of pain? Well, Danni, we are going to let you answer your own questions. Just what have you gained from these relationships you deemed so terrible? Can you answer the question? Well, let me help you.

What have you learned from your mother? You have learned not to hate your children. You have learned that everyone deserves a hug—a good reason why you hug your children so much—because you didn't get hugs from your mother. You knew how much you craved them and how much you wanted one, and you couldn't get them from your mom and dad. You most certainly were going to make sure that your kids got this. What else did you learn from your mother? Well, you learned that meanness is ugly. You learned that hatred is ugly and leaves big scars. You learned that all is not as it seems, that the eye is not always the window to the soul—you believe that your mother has an ugly soul, yet her eyes do not reveal this. You also learned that love is not always enough—you know that your father loved you, that he has attempted, in his feeble way, to show you, yet that has not been enough.

What did you learn from your tumultuous marriage? Again, you learned that you are strong—strong enough to know you are more worthy than the abuse heaped on you, strong enough to know that this man is not good for you, strong enough to know that God did protect you through that relationship, and strong enough to know that God guided you out of that relationship.

God has always been by your side. He chose the very best for you when he chose all four spirit guides for you. He knew, as you knew, that this life was a hard one—one wherein you chose to move forward, maybe faster than necessary, considering all that has been heaped on you. But through all the bad, God has also blessed you with good. He has blessed you with three beautiful children—not always nice, not always considerate or kind, but nevertheless they are your pride and joy. You always wonder if maybe you could have done just a little better with those kids, but you did your very best, and as you watch these children mature—albeit it may take time—when you see the maturity, you will begin to take great pride in them and say "See, God, they did turn out okay."

Your purpose in this life was to understand that not all that comes from God is good, *but* it is meant to be. It is meant to be so that you can see that not all people are good, but not all people are bad. You are meant to know that love can be given even if it isn't received. You are meant to know that you can be nice to people even if they aren't nice to you. You are meant to know that there is bad in this world, but there is also good; that there is sadness, but there is happiness; that there is loneliness, but there is also friendship to bring you joy—friends to help you laugh, to bring you happiness, and to lift you from your problems, even if it is just for a short while.

Give yourself love, Danni. If there is no one around to love you, then love yourself. If there is no one around you to take you for lunch, then take yourself. If there is no one around you to go to a movie with, go with yourself. For God made you whole, and he made you full—full of love and caring, full of kindness and joy, full of happiness and laughter. He gave you a light heart to help you through your burdens, but you have fallen victim to a heavy heart caught up in the tribulations heaped on you, and you have forgotten how to laugh, how to skip, how to have a joyful heart. All you need, Danni, is to recapture your joyful heart, to count your blessings, name them one by one, and see that they outnumber your tribulations by many—by many, many more.

You are a beautiful, vibrant woman just entering your best years. You have done all your hard work. Now you can find your joyful heart once more to capture your joy and peace, and once you find this heart that brings you all that you need to pursue happiness, you will see doors swing wide open. Because a joyful heart is attractive; a heavy heart is not—a heart full of laughter is contagious; a sad heart is not. All that you crave and all that you dream for is invested in your heart. Make your dreams come true by giving in to the lure of your heart. Give up the pain, give up the hurt, give up the regrets, and give up the resentment, and move into this glorious world God has waiting for you.

Do something you have always wanted to do but have never had the courage on your own. Join a choir. You love to sing. Give that voice a chance to soar. Let it lift you out of this depression or this feeling of being unloved you have found yourself in. That is all you need to turn your life into the success story you crave. You are well loved by God, well protected by God, and well guided by your spirit guides. You have all that is necessary to move forward. Forget the past. It is behind, meant to be forgotten, meant to be left behind, meant to be buried, to rot in the ground. Take the time to write all your woes. Don't miss a one, because you don't want any of them lingering with you. Once you have written them all down on a piece of paper, bury them in the ground, deep. Then out of anything, make a tombstone that says "Here lie the woes of Danni, buried and gone forever."

Now your most pressing question, Danni: "Why didn't your mother ever love you?" Have you ever asked her if she loves you? Maybe you should. You might be surprised by her answer. This is your last hard quest ahead of you, and then it is clear sailing. You need to ask your mother this question, you need to insist on an answer, and you must come to grips with her answer and then put it behind you with all your other woes. Take the time to also ask your dad why he allowed it?

Danni, you are worthy of this answer, and God wants you to know this answer because he loves you and he wants only happiness for you. But until you take on this one last mission, happiness will evade you, so please God and please yourself—find out the answer and then bring this answer to God so that he too can blow it into the wind!

Praise you, Danni, for pursuing, for persevering, and for continuing on with a battle you haven't always felt was worth it. Take the time to praise God. He would appreciate it. Take the time to sing his praises as you begin on this journey that will lead you to happiness.

My dear Lord Jesus, thank you for all your blessings. Thank you, my Lord! Lord, do you have a message for my good friend Michelle? Thank you, Lord.

* * *

Dear Barbara,

There is a message for your friend Michelle. As you know, my child, there is always a message, always guidance for those who choose to follow the wisdom of their Lord, their Creator.

* * *

Dear Michelle, my precious child, a child that tries so hard to please me and everyone around you. Are you getting tired, my child? Are you growing weary?

It is a very difficult life to try to please everyone, especially when some people in your life are hard to please, but, Michelle, you keep trying and trying and trying and trying.

Michelle, what if it were okay to quit trying so hard? What if you had my permission to quit trying so hard? Michelle, I am well pleased with you my child. I do not want you to wear yourself out trying to please other people. I am very proud of you my child. You no longer have to work so hard to ensure I am happy with you.

Michelle, my child, my precious, precious child, just be. Michelle, just be! You are a caring, compassionate individual just as I intended you to be. You no longer have to keep trying to be all those things you already are. Take a break, my child, and just take care of Michelle for a while.

Michelle, can you change your sister's illness? No, you cannot. Michelle, can you change your husband's disposition? No, you cannot. Michelle, my daughter, you now have very little influence in your sons' lives, so let go. You are already there. You have already achieved all that I ever wanted for you, my child. You have grown into the woman who makes me proud. You are all that you were meant to be, so now, my child, you no longer have to keep trying to please me and all the people around you, from the busboy to your manager to your husband.

You please me greatly, and now I want you to please yourself. The solitary walks in the morning that you love, take time to do them. Lunch with your friends, time with your family—whatever pleases you is what I want for you.

Just be—you ask what that means. Michelle, I will tell you what it means. It means it is okay to have negative thoughts—you are human. It is okay to have a judgment—you are human. It is okay to sleep in on Saturday morning—you are human.

Michelle, quit criticizing yourself. You are just as I had hoped you would be. You are there, my child. You are at the point in your life where you can do as you like, think the thoughts you want, and know "Guess what? My God thinks I am okay, my God is proud of me, and my God thinks I have achieved all that he put in my path. If my God thinks I am okay, then I must be okay."

Let go, my child, of all and any criticism. Once again I tell you, you are exactly where I want you to be, and it is now time to enjoy your life. Do what brings you enjoyment not the others around you. It is okay to say "No, that doesn't work for me, but you go ahead and enjoy yourself. I have other plans." It is okay to stand up for yourself and do the things that make you happy. Try it, my child. You might like it, and remember you have my permission to just be how you are.

Go forward my child, and love life!

Your Loving God

My dear Lord Jesus, Cindy would like a message from you, my Lord. Thank you, Lord, for your faithfulness, thank you.

* * *

Dear Barbara,

My child, my child, put away your fear this letter may not meet Cindy's needs. Any letter from me is a blessing, and anyone who receives a letter from me will benefit from it, so write and share your beautiful gift.

* * *

Dear Cindy,

My child, my love—yes, you are my love, a creature of God, a creature of love, and a creature of giving. You are a great lady who gives and expects little in return. Cindy, you have always been a child of God, and I know of your great love for me.

Thank you Cindy, for your faithfulness, and thank you for sharing my love. That is all I really ask of my children—to spread my love, spread *God's* love, and we are all capable of doing this just with very small acts of kindness each day.

You, Cindy, my faithful and loving servant, have been doing this for many years, and I'm very proud of you! Where do you go from here, you ask? Well, Cindy, where would you like to go from here? Do you want to continue working as hard as you do, which gives you great value, or do you want to slow down, take things easy, and enjoy your retirement? The choice is yours because with either decision there will be losses and there will be gains.

The loss in slowing down would be that you would not feel as valued, as needed as you do right now. The gain would be that you would be less tired—you know, Cindy, the bone-crunching tiredness that covers your whole body—and you would also have more time to spend with your husband, your love, your very best friend.

Which sounds better to you? In your heart, you know there will never be enough years for you and your husband to be together. Why not enjoy the ones you do have? Maybe take a small trip, the two of you. Maybe do a crossword puzzle together. Maybe read to your husband. Whatever it is you decide, Cindy, it will be fine with me because you see, my child, I just want what is best for you, and when you truly search your heart and make the right decision for yourself, it will be the right decision for me.

Your girls are fine, Cindy, I am very proud of both your daughters as I know you are. You and your husband did a wonderful job raising these girls to love their God and to fight against injustice in this world. Good job, my loyal and faithful servant, good job!

Cindy, all is well in your life. Your family is happy, and they love and serve me. Continue on as you have been, my child, knowing that I approve and am happy with how you have chosen to live your life.

Your Loving God

Dearest Lord, as I write tonight and question the emotion my friend Darlene is going through, I ask, Precious Lord, for a message for my friend Darlene, to help her understand her thoughts, her emotions, her prayers, and her pleas. I ask, Lord, that you bring my friend Darlene some rest to her thoughts, some rest for her feelings, and some rest for her soul. Bring solace and peace to her body as she tries to heal her aches, both internal and external, as she tries to placate her emotions, as she soothes them with food. Lord, please help her understand.

* * *

My dearest child, my dearest little child, your concern for others is admirable. Your love for others is commendable, and as you ask for guidance and understanding for your friend, I want you to understand that your need is also great. Your need for love and understanding is also important, and I ask that you put prayer and meditation into what you need and what you want.

And you, my dearest child Darlene—you who run from your own wants, who run from your own needs, who puts the needs of all others before your own—you, my dearest child, are your own worst enemy as you struggle with the fight between mind and body. You are determined that the mind will win at all costs, that the mind will win over all else at the cost of health, at the cost of emotional sanctuary, at the cost of your own wants and needs. You believe that you must not give in to your needs, you must not give in to your wants, you must not acknowledge or even believe that your wants are different for the heart than the mind, because you would then need to consider believing in the feelings of the heart. You would then have to believe in the need for more, and you, my dear child, are very afraid of rocking the boat. You, my dear child, are afraid that if you rock the boat, it will tip, you will fall out and drown, and then there is no turning back. And that is your very worst fear—not being able to turn back should you want to—for if you were left out alone without the support and protection that you believe you need to survive, you believe that you are not able to stand on your own. You believe you would be ostracized and ridiculed for making decisions that don't always have the best interest of the family at heart, when all you really want right now are what the best interests for your heart are. What are the best interests that would bring you the sanctity that you crave yet not rock the boat of your family. You aren't even willing to cause a ripple in the water, and this, my beautiful friend, is what is causing your stress.

You don't get it. You pray, read your Bible, and worship God, and all you ask for in return is some peace of mind. You have fulfilled your covenant to God, and you have stayed married for life. That is your true commitment to God—to follow that rule, that law, that commandment, that covenant, stay with the same man till death do you part. That is your personal commitment to self and God, and now why can't God just give you some peace? That is all you ask for—peace of mind. Yet every time you believe you have been given this precious gift, the gift of peacefulness, you feel a nagging, you feel a pulling, you feel a tugging at your heart, and again the battle begins. It is very easy to tell your mind what you are going to do, but it's not so easy telling your heart—your aching heart, your bruised heart, your heart that feels all the pain of feeling unloved, your heart that carries all that hidden pain of feeling inadequate, not measuring up, not needing the ties that binds, just needing the precious gift of unconditional and unrelenting love. You just want to feel loved. So much of the time, you feel used—used by everyone, used by all your family. Can they not see that you have needs? Can they not notice that you also have needs? It seems to you that you give, give, give, and give, and nothing seems to come back in return. When is it your time to receive?

I tell you verily, Darlene, unless you let your family know what your needs are, they won't know. Until you identify your needs to yourself and then to them, they will never know what your needs are.

Do not be afraid. Do not be afraid to stand up for yourself and declare yourself as also having needs. Do not be afraid to stand up for yourself and declare what you want.

Do not feel guilty for having needs, you were born having needs, and that fact has not changed. All my creatures have needs. That is part of the human element, and you, my precious child, are human. You were born human, and you remain human, with humanly needs. Do not ignore these needs, for these needs were placed upon you for your own personal growth.

Please do not ignore these needs. I want you to understand that when you stand up for yourself and declare your needs, you will feel strong and fulfilled. You will feel rewarded and awarded the special gift of feeling important, heard, understood, and loved, for when you ignore your own needs, you are withholding love, your own personal love for self. It is very dangerous and harmful to withhold personal love for oneself—this causes illnesses, unhappiness, and a tarnishing to the personal self.

I have made all my children worthy of self-love. I have made all my children worthy of love that comes from within. For some, this is the hardest part of their life—unveiling their personal love. For you, my dearest child, I tell you again: your unveiling is now; your belief in self is now, your need for personal love is now, and so I ask you to reflect on your needs. I ask that you close your eyes and imagine your needs being fulfilled. And now I ask you to explain the difference in how you feel. Can you go back to the old feelings? Can you return to the pent-up depression you feel from not honoring your wants? I don't think so.

I know your fear of this very, very hard task of releasing your frustration and anger, but I also know the freedom it allows to bring this need to rest.

Start small, with one small need, and work up to bigger needs and allow the blossoming to begin. Watch the respect you gain from your family. Feel the love as you begin to stand up for your wants.

I know you well, child, as I hear you say "But I don't have any wants. I don't have any needs. What is he talking about?" but I tell you, dear child, you do have wants. You do have needs as all do. You must uncover these wants, you must uncover these needs, and you must set them free for you to find the ultimate happiness you crave, to find the ultimate peace you crave. As you remember me in your prayers, I ask that you believe in this information I share with your friend. Believe and put your efforts into releasing stress, pain, fear, and agony just by acknowledging and believing that you are also worthy of honoring your needs, because you are.

Dear Precious Lord, would you please answer a question for Sharon? Her question is "Why do I have such a hard time letting go, and will I ever be able to do the big surrender?" Precious Lord, praise you for your love that you have for all. Amen.

* * *

Dearest Beverley, you bring a question to me from a lady you have never met, a lady who has her own fears and her own concerns for her life. A lady who tries hard to be all that she can, all that she believes she is supposed to be, yet as she struggles with all that she has determined she is meant to be, she begins to find herself lost. Lost in all that she is caught up in as she is struggling with these important missions to her. But some of them are just for her, some of them are not meant to bring me glory. Nor are they meant to bring her glory—all they bring for this lady who struggles is heartache. She is trying hard to be all that she should be, but what she is forgetting is that she is already all that she is meant to be. She is already all that I want her to be as she tries so hard when it is not necessary. She tries so hard when, truly, it is only causing her to feel drained, unsuccessful, and exhausted, all in her attempt to be able to claim that she is all that I have wanted.

This is not what I want for this lady Sharon. This is not what I want for her, to feel too drained to continue. What I want is joyfulness, what I want is soulfulness, what I want is rejoicing and clapping of hands in celebration of life—just life, just the claiming of life—because without life, there is no opportunity for laughter. Without life, there is no opportunity for happiness and fun and excitement and cheerfulness and the glee that comes with doing all those things that make you happy, all those things that put the life into your soul.

You don't do these things anymore, Sharon. You don't do the things that make your heart sing, you don't do the things that make your soul sing, and you don't do the things that make your mind sing as you go whizzing by on your rollerblades and feel the wind blow through your hair. Do you remember how you used to feel so close to me when you were outdoors, enjoying the day by feeling my presence everywhere you went? Do you remember how close you used to feel to me when you would take to the outdoors and just enjoy, to feel the present, to live in the present, to hear your soul sing to you as you hurried along a path in a good clip just to feel energized, just to feel fueled for the day? What happened to those moments? What happened to our time alone? What happened to our harmonious relationship? For it no longer exists, it no longer belongs to the two of us because you are way too busy working on being the best you can be, you are way too busy working on this new person you are trying to see in the mirror. But what happened to the old person I created? What happened to the old person I had planted on this earth? I don't see her anymore. She has all but disappeared, and I miss her.

How about you, Sharon, do you miss this old person who used to take time to stop, bend down, and smell the flowers as they bloomed? What happened to this old person who took time to talk to the people on the street that she passed? What happened to this person who loved to laze around and just feel lazy? I haven't seen this person for a while, and I find myself missing the Sharon I created.

This new Sharon, she is of your creation—she is of your mold, not of mine, for the Sharon I created was meant to enjoy life. She was meant to surrender to the love of nature. She was meant to soften to the voice on the street. This new Sharon pursues her best and has forgotten that she truly has left her best behind her. I want you to find the best Sharon we both love. I want you to go in pursuit of where you have left her, pull her out, dust her off, and take her everywhere with you, for she is truly the Sharon of love, the Sharon of caring, the Sharon of knowing, and the Sharon of pure heart, gentle touch, and kind life. Find her.

Now you question why you can't do the big surrender. What big surrender? What big surrender would you be talking about? The surrender of your past, the surrender of your history, the surrender of who you are and what has made you, the surrender of what has shaped you and defined you, the surrender that has taught wisdom and strength of character—is that the big surrender you believe is pulling you down? Well, I have news for you: this is not pulling you down but is instead making you the strong, reliable, confident woman you have become today. For if you had made the big surrender, had you been able to let go, both in memory and in heart—had you been able to let go, not thought about any of your changes, directions, decisions, and commitments— what would you have learned, what would you have retained to guide you today? I daresay nothing—I daresay absolutely nothing, and how much wiser would you be today?

These are now the questions that need to be answered, because you are who you are. You are who you have become because of what you have held onto, from what you have learned from, from what you have made choices—wise choices to ensure that the same lesson did not need to be learned over twice. Had it been easy to let go, to do the big surrender, then what lessons would have been learned? Do you see my point?

I want to tell you a little bit about why God made you the way he did. Because he wanted you to think, reflect, mull over your decisions. He wanted you to believe his purpose and to believe his guidance, and through all, that has led you to your Lord, and to all that has led you to your station in life, your position in life, and your grace in life has been through the ability to look back and reflect on how things could have and would have been done differently. As you reflect and as you believe and as you choose this new path, it is always influenced by what had led you to this new path.

The letting go is truly a real curse for you, for you don't want to let go—you don't want to let go of something that was so important to you. You never want to see yourself as a failure or as someone who has failed at anything, but what I want you to do is put yourself back into a place that leaves you with the least pain. Now follow that path. Feel the lack of pain and feel the lack of growth and understanding, and now tell me, would you rather truly be on that other path, or would you rather work through the pain and be where you are today? For with each pain does come growth and understanding, and with each pain does come the breath of fresh air and new beginnings and new starts. With new starts come new gains, and with new gains come new accomplishments. And with new accomplishments come the success that we crave—the success of learning, the success of knowing, and the success of winning the rights and privileges of knowing ourselves just a little better.

I want you to remember who you were and who you are, and ask the question "Would I give up the pain and anguish to be that person again?" If your answer is no, you do not want to be who that person was but prefer to be who this person is. Then, you now have your answer.

My dear Lord Jesus, do you have a message for my sister, Lord, a message of hope and cheer—a message that will help her move forward? Move her forward with her life, move her forward with her job, move her forward Lord to find peace and happiness. Thank you, my Lord, thank you.

* * *

Dear Barbara,

Your sister is very sad right now, trying to find her place of belonging, her place of value and her place of liking just who she is at this moment. Who is Beverley? Who is this very special creature created in the image of her God?

* * *

Dear Beverley,

You are my child! You are a child of God, a perfect creation that is holy, and, Beverley, you are mine!

I love you dearly, and I want for you to be happy. I want you to rejoice, and I want you to be thankful. Be happy Bev, that you have been given a loving and caring family. Rejoice Bev, that all your family is healthy and independent.

Beverley, I have given you all things to make your life a happy one. I have given you a family that loves you, I have given you friends who love you, I have given you privilege and wealth, and I have given you health to enjoy all my gifts. Rejoice, Beverley, rejoice and give thanks for the gifts of your Lord.

Should you retire? You know the answer to that question, my dear child. You know what your life would be like. Do not count yourself short, my dear child. You are needed at your place of employment, you are respected at your place of employment, and there are friends at your place of employment.

Yes, Beverley, you are right. There will never be a friend like Susan, but look around you. Take time to scan your surroundings. There are friends who are just waiting for you to ask them for coffee. If you feel unsure after all these years of working for your employer, how do other ladies feel? Look around, my child. There are women in your place of employment who need your encouragement. They need your leadership, and yes, Bev, they too need a friend.

Let go of the sadness and start giving thanks for the very good paying job that you do have, thanks for the short commute, and thanks that you work at a place that has allowed you to move up the rungs of success. Yes, Beverley, you have been very successful! You have worked hard, and you have been rewarded with monetary gain and rewarded with respect for the way you lead the women you supervise.

The sadness is caused because you choose to concentrate on what you don't have instead of what you do have. Give thanks, my child, give thanks! List them one by one, all the great gifts that you received in this lifetime.

Your weight, you ask. Are you growing weary of obsessing about your weight? I believe your words are "That which we resist will persist." Let go, my child. Love yourself for who you are, not what you look like. You are a caring woman who comes to all those in need. You are a wonderful wife, a marvelous mother, a grand, grand grandmother, a fabulous friend, and a niece who always, always comes to an aunt in need.

You are a beautiful, kind, loving, caring human being who will be much happier and energetic when she realizes who she is and forgets about who she is not.

Let go, my child. Let go and let God! Let God decide about your weight. Let God decide about your energy. Let God decide where he wants you to be and how you shall get there, and come along for the ride. Enjoy the ride, Bev. Don't miss it, because I know if you let go, you will have the time of your life on this ride called life journey.

Let go, my child, and know that I am very proud of you. I love you just the way you are, and in the end, that is all that really matters.

Let go, my child, and hang on for the ride of a lifetime.

Your Loving God

Dear Precious Lord, I know you feel my loneliness and my hurt and my feelings of not being loved as I have spent so many years living through my children, for my children, and I don't know how to change to live just for me. Can you help me, Lord?

* * *

Dearest Beverley, yes, you do hurt. Yes, you do cry tears of pain, tears of hurt, tears of caring, and tears of loving. What you truly want to ask is how can you stop loving instead of loving, how can you put all your energy into not loving instead of into loving. How can you center yourself around yourself instead of around all of those you care about, always giving more than you have to give? Always loving more than you have to love, yet giving it away and leaving your bank empty, leaving yourself with nothing to replenish, nothing to fill yourself up with when the reservoir is empty, and not knowing where to turn when you feel so drained of love and caring. With no one else to turn to because you don't know anyone else who gives it all away.

How can you begin to believe that you don't have to give it all away to be loved, you don't need to give it all away to know that you are liked? For it is very hard for anyone to like you when you struggle with liking yourself, it is very hard for anyone to care when you have drained yourself and there is nothing left to care about. How can you begin to give away something you don't have to give away? How can you begin to leave others with what you don't have to leave?

It is very hard because you then begin to try and capture it from others, and they are not willing to give it away, and you are then in a struggle to try and capture what is not yours to capture.

How can you learn to leave your bank full? How can you remember to prepare for what you term a rainy day? Give, Bev, give to yourself as you give to others. Allow yourself to love yourself. Give yourself all the attention you would shower on others.

Believe that you are worthy of love, that you are worthy of being loved, and understand that no one—I mean *no one*—can love you like you can and know that no one can feel your pain like you can and no one can comfort you like you can, because you and only you are in charge of all that comes in and all that goes out. So know that you are able to conquer your own demons and you are able to live your own life through self-love, self-respect, self-care, self-understanding, and self-life, for this is your life and only your life to live. Now please live it for you and not for everyone else around you.

Precious Lord, would you please answer a question for my good friend Noreen? Part 1 of her question is what is needed for her to complete her renewal, to completely recover, to completely transform into her authentic self? And part 2, how can Darren and her work better together? Or how does she support his transformation into his authentic self? Praise you, Lord, for being there, and thank you for loving me, just me, for who I am. Amen.

* * *

Beverley, a harder question than you are used to receiving. Let me guide you through the answers for your dear friend Noreen. Noreen is on track. She has worked hard to prepare herself for all that is ahead of her. As she pursues her career in healing, she will be rewarded with many wondrous events, full of good and happiness, transformations in patients, and the opportunity to witness God in action. She loves what she does, yet finds herself exhausted at the end of the day—a hard thing for her when she likes to have the energy to putter around, play with her animals and enjoy her husband. This, at present, is not happening, and through this, Noreen is losing sight of her authentic self as she is very aware. She has been putting so much energy into all she does to support and lift her clients that there is nothing left for her at the end of the day. She needs her alone time—time to reenergize, time to claim herself, and at this time in her life, it is missing. It is not something easy for her to reclaim because she is a dedicated professional, giving all she has and all that comes to her in the form of energy to her clients. She is so thankful to be able to support this that she forgets about Noreen—the Noreen that God chose to be the little spitfire that she is, the Noreen God chose to follow him as she searches for her personal meaning.

Noreen does not need to search any further. She has found the Noreen whom God created to be a child of God, to love him, to worship him, and to thank him for all he has given her. She is a special child of God because she has been loyal to him, through different beliefs, through different religions, through different societies, she has never lost touch with who her God is and that, through all the layers, he is always available to her. She, like all, gets frustrated with her God when, in fact, this is just a matter of forgetting to take the time she needs with her God.

Noreen's answer to her question is so simple, so easy. Just take time to be with God to become her authentic self. No magic, no tricks—just spend the time she needs to get reenergized with God. He is the source—he is the abundant source of energy, and it is available for all. They need only ask. She has forgotten to ask for her daily dose of energy as she hurries about meeting the needs of all around her. She has neglected her own need.

Noreen, you know me—you know me well. You just haven't taken the time to reacquaint yourself. You barely take time to acknowledge me these days. I can't support you or lift you if you don't ask for my help.

Child of mine, come to me. Take the time to sit with me. Take the time to see me all around you. You are now in such a peaceful, relaxing place without the hustle and bustle of the big city, but you haven't taken the time to see me, haven't taken the time to see me all around—in the water, so close, that you love; in the air you breathe, in the flowers you like to bring into your house. I am here, Noreen. I am close. I never leave your side. Please take the time for me. I will fill you with all you lack to bring you to this place you refer to as your authentic self. I prefer to call it your place with God, the place where you come to fill my presence into your soul, the place you come to fill your soul with your connection with me, to soar in my love, to feel me on your face as the sun beats down, to feel me on your back as the wind blows you forward, to feel me as the rain pelts down. You need, Noreen, to take the time to come, to relax in my presence, to fill your starving body of my presence. I am always here, always ready to give you what you need to become your authentic self.

Now you ask about Darren, a man you love dearly, a man you have chosen to guide to his own destiny, but my dear child, you cannot guide anyone to their destiny. You again refer to this as his authentic self, but you truly want to ensure that Darren is on the right path to his destiny. That is not your job, Noreen. That's mine. Don't try to do my job for me. Right now you are overwhelmed with what is your job.

Darren is stalled. He is in no movement as he searches for who he is. He struggles with believing that he could be loved by God. Why would God love him? His own mother wasn't even capable of that. When you don't believe you are worthy of God's love, you then starve yourself of all that brings you the reasoning and purpose of an individual destiny. How can I help Darren to recognize I love him? Well, I start by giving him the opportunity of rising each day. He takes this for granted, but he shouldn't, even that small gift comes from me. Is that hard for you to believe? It shouldn't be, because you give thanks for it. Darren has caught himself in a void, struggling to find his way out, struggling to determine his purpose. He puts way too much energy into trying to determine his purpose when his purpose is to be Darren. This has all been planned as he and I prepared him for this world. He has agreed to be caught in this void as he comes to grips with why. He will come out of it stronger, wiser, and more supportive.

Have patience. To you this seems like such a long time, when in reality, it is such a short period in his long life. The purpose of this void is known to Darren—perhaps not on a conscious level, but it is known to him. He will survive, he will prosper, and he will become this man God created him to be, all in his time and all in my time.

Noreen, take good care of yourself, give yourself love, and give yourself some time, and you will then become your authentic self.

I love you!

God

Lord Jesus,

For years my sister has been writing letters to God for me, and now I would like to write a letter to God for her. Lord do you have a message for my sister, my womb mate, and my greatest defender?

* * *

Of course I have a message for your sister, the sister you know is always in your corner defending and carrying you.

* * *

Dear Bev,

There is a lot of pressure for your sister to write this letter. How will she ever be able to hear our voices like you do? How will she ever be able to write a letter for someone like her sister does? Will this letter be good enough? Will it have meaning for her sister? Now two sisters with the same gift—what will this mean for these two sisters, mirror twins, different in every way but now with the same gift? How will these girls deal with the competition? Because it has always been a competition for the Munro girls—which is thinner, which is prettier, which is smarter. Now which one will write the best letters?

My oh my, what now? What will happen to these two sisters who love each other so much but still want to be better than the other? It is time to put away the comparing, time to put away the envy. Yes, you both are pretty. Yes, you both will lose weight. It does not matter if Barb is two pounds less. It does not matter if Bev has prettier hair. It matters that these two sisters work together with the beautiful gift that God has given them. What a treasure for friends to have a letter from God written by twin sisters. Yes, write together, one from Bev and one from Barb.

You both will have an income from your gift, but remember to give of your gift. A gift is to be shared, so share freely of the most precious of gifts. Friends and family treasure these letters, and yes, you have broken ground for your sister. You did have to deal with ridicule for your gift, and the path you blazed has made it much easier for your sister, but that is what big sisters do, blaze a path for the little sister.

Bev, pick up on Barb's enthusiasm and write more, not only for the benefit of family and friends, but for your benefit also, for when you write, you are entering the ethereal world where you communicate with the angels. Fly with the angels, Bev, and you can do this every day by writing a letter—maybe a small one for yourself, maybe a larger one for a friend, or maybe in conjunction with your sister—for no other reason than you can.

Publish a book, *Letters by Twins*. Your sister has always thought these letters should be available for the benefit of others. You have many letters that will benefit the masses. Your future is bright, and your retirement will bring you joy and the energy that you have craved for so long. Enjoy your husband, enjoy your children, enjoy your grandchildren and most of all, enjoy your life. As you know, we are always with you, and you used to engage us in conversation often. Start again. We love you so much. We want to visit with you, guide you, and cheer you up when you are sad. Reach out to us. We are always by your side.

Your angels

Dear Precious Lord,

I ask for a letter, the annual letter for my sister's birthday, as she has had so much turmoil in her life. I just ask that you bring her a clear message of hope and love and happiness to allow her the freedom to move forward, as she plans for the next segment of her life. I ask that you fill her with your love, encouragement, and faith that you have the ultimate plan for her. Precious Lord, again I thank you and praise you for the beautiful gift you have blessed me with.

* * *

Dearest Beverley, I have a message for both you and your sister. I have a message of love and beauty for two ladies who truly know how to love and give to others. Two sisters made in my image to relay messages of truth and love, to guide others, to be able to allow self-love, self-belief, and self-attention that is missing in so many people. Continue to write, continue to love, and continue to be loved, all in my name.

* * *

Dearest Barbara, my little Barbara, always waiting for a warm embrace of my arms, always waiting for the touch of my hand, always waiting for the message from God before proceeding, so trusting, so loyal, so fruitful. I again praise you and thank you for your loyalty, always putting me first in all things, such a child of God. You are truly blessed, my child, you are truly blessed and protected under my light.

So what questions can I answer for you today my precious child? What questions could I possibly answer that you haven't already asked and received the answer to?

As you move into your senior years, know that life will only get better and better for you. As you lean toward the last part of life, know that you will find much ease and relaxation. Your push to succeed will be met. Your need to be supported in all you do will be met. Your need and ability to support all that you meet will also be met. You will be able to breeze into retirement with a smile on your face, knowing all is well. You have done well. You will have given all you could give, knowing that you are a precious child of God—like all his other children, knowing you are loved.

Again you question the word love and the many different facets of love. What does it mean? What does the word love mean? Well, my little child, let me shed even more light on the word love.

Love is the purpose and being of all living objects. Love is the purpose and being of life and living and being. Love builds the world, and yet love can also destroy it. Love means many different things to many different people, but love is the one and only fuel of the world.

Love brings you the breath that keeps you alive, and love brings you the energy to function. Love is the all-powerful emotion of human life not only on earth but also on every universe, and that is because love is my language, the only language created by me. All other languages were created by man, but my language was created by me.

Every being is taught my language before being conceived, and every living being is given this language to share at will; however, what seems to happen is that my language seems to get forgotten for other languages. As my subjects, my people, start to grow, they forget my language for the other languages of fear, greed, jealously to only mention a few, as they can't seem to retain my language, the language of their birth. This is when the earth begins to struggle. This is when the earth feels the pressures of war, poverty, homelessness, selfishness, self-centeredness, and all the serious ill effects of forgetting their mother tongue, their language of love.

My dear child, the best thing you can do for me is to speak my language, to remember to speak my language every day and every minute of every day. For when you speak my language, you will be healed of all ailments, you will be healed of all hurts and misunderstandings, because when speaking my language, the other languages of the world—the languages of greed, bullying, meanness, selfishness—cannot sustain themselves. They cannot live or survive when my language becomes the dominant language.

My language is the easiest language in the world to learn because it was given to you at birth. It was your birthing gift from me. It did not need to be learned because it was already present. All that I asked was that it was spoken every day to keep it fresh and abundant in both your heart and your mind—the two most important and functional parts of the body, as both are full of thought and emotion and both fuel the body on how it should proceed. Both the head and the heart speak the language of love, and this was part of my great plan of ensuring that the language of love was always housed inside the body.

So when searching for answers and trusting that it is the mind that is going to bring all the answers, that is not so. The heart is just as powerful as the brain to answer all questions of the body. The heart is just as available as the mind. The heart, most times, just has a quieter side. It takes more intuition to listen to the heart when the mind races from thought to thought, so when waiting for the answer from the heart, you must find a way to escape from the barrage of thoughts always running through the mind. Be still, be silent, and be one with me to hear the messages of the heart. Sometimes they will be the same as the mind, but many times, the heart will bring a different message with a different perspective, and this is where the phrase "Follow your heart" came from. For the heart talks slower, it talks quieter, and it talks the truth.

Always follow your heart, Barbara. Always follow your heart.

Dear Precious Lord, a question from my friend Louise, whose question for you is "What is your will on where I am to serve you? I want to be obedient." Precious Lord would you please answer this question for Louise, praise you, Precious Lord.

* * *

Dearest Beverley, as you write for a lady who has accepted and embraced her family of choice—a family she chose to accept, chose to embrace, chose to love—as you write for this lady, write with love, write with devotion, and write with the will of acceptance and understanding of all things and all people.

Louise, you bring much to your Lord, you bring much to your church, and you bring much to your community. You are accepted and appreciated as you pursue the needs of supporting a family, as you work hard to maintain the style necessary to bring peace and relaxation into your life, but as you work hard for your survival, you are still working for your Lord, you are still serving your Lord, you are still perfecting all that he asked of you. You, Louise McDougall, do God's will each day. You make sure that all of God's creatures are loved. Do you understand, Louise McDougall, what your Lord is telling you? Do you understand what you do each day that is God's will—that is serving your Lord, your God, your Savior? Do you understand that each day that you get up and prepare yourself for work, you are preparing to again do your Lord's request of you?

As you prepare to enter your place of work, as you prepare to build the courage to return each day to this place of work, I want you to remember just this one little thing: you are serving your Lord. You are serving your God. You are fulfilling your own prophesy, and you are completing a request God asked of you long before you chose this life on earth. You, Louise, are bringing some happiness to old men.

You, Louise, are bringing a smile to the faces of old men. You, Louise, allow them a lightness as they continue on with their day. You are bringing each and every one of these gentlemen a feeling of beginning, a feeling of renewing, a feeling of belonging, and a feeling of family—a family that can meet for a very short time and then move on to other parts of their lives. But this is a family, as God gives each and every one of us many families to nurture. You, Louise, have been given this family to nurture. You have been given this family to bring to a point of accepting and preparing. And you, Louise, have been given to this family to love—to love unconditionally, to love undeniably, to love with enthusiasm, and to love from the heart.

Not always easy, as you have to sometimes discipline, sometimes scold. Sometimes even you must be the one to ask them to leave the family for short times, but you, Louise, always fill them with your love. You fill them with your laughter, and you fill them with your caring and concern for each and every one of them. This, Louise, is serving your Lord. This, Louise, is doing God's plan for you. This, Louise, is serving all that God expects from you. This is truly doing God's work. This is truly serving all that God requests from you.

You have taken the love of God, and you have spread this love to all his people. You have taken this love and shared it with God's creatures. All that God expects of you and all that God wants from you is to share this love—the love of God, the love of Jesus, given to you to share, given to you to give away, given to you to be shared with all who surround you. Again, an easy task, a simple task, but a task that is very important, a task that creates great energy in the place that we go to rest, in the place we go to gain peace—the place that we go to reunite with our Creator. You, Louise you, are making that place a better place with the energy that is ignited by the love you share.

So continue to love all of those old codgers. Continue to give them affection and attention, and continue to know that you are doing God's will, you are living his purpose for you, you are following the plan, and you are being given the opportunity to do God's work.

God's work does not just take place in churches or in places of worship, but God's work takes place wherever God resides, and God resides in you, Louise, so take great pride in knowing that your Lord is very pleased with you. He is very pleased with your desire to please him, and your God is very pleased with your desire to work for him. You do work for your Lord, Louise. Every day you work for him, every day you serve him, and every day you are fulfilling his will for you. So remember to share your love, share it with everyone, but especially share it with all of those old codgers who choose to huddle at your place of work, who choose to gather at your place of work, and know if they were not there, if they ceased to come, you would no longer be able to serve your Lord. So go with love, go with trust, and go with the faith of the Lord, confident in your belief and confident in your direction, confident in your trust and confident in all that God provides. For it is God that provides all, it is God who serves all, and it is God who loves all!

My dear lord Jesus, do you have a message for my dear friend Brenda? Thank you, my Lord.

* * *

Dear Barbara,

Of course, there is a message for your friend Brenda, a woman with great compassion and courage, a woman with much wisdom and fortitude. Always there is a message for the people who want to hear.

* * *

Dear Brenda,

My child, you are a child of God, a child much loved and much appreciated for all the kindness and love you spread around your small town. My dear Brenda, I am very proud of you and the unconditional love that you show so many.

My child, my child, always you are under my protection, and I want you to always remember that! Brenda, I am here to protect you, I am here to watch over you, and I am here for you to always bring your problems to. My child, I hear every one of your urgings, every one of your pleas, and every one of your desperate callings. I am here, my child. I am here to support you through everything as you are *always* there to support all your friends. I will never forsake you or forget you.

Brenda, you witness me every day in your early morning runs as you see the sun come up in the sky. Who do you think has placed that sun in just the right position to warm you, to give you light? Brenda, who is it that places the birds in the trees and the butterflies in the air? As you know, my child, you cannot create a bird, you cannot create a butterfly, only your loving God and Savior is able to put these beautiful creatures on your earth for your pleasure Brenda, for your benefit and for your joy as you run your path each morning. Brenda, know that I am very proud of you, for as you know well, my child, there is only love. Nothing else matters in my world. So as you work so very hard to earn the income that you believe will bring you security, know that the only important thing for me is that you continue to spread your love all around.

You are a very special person who uses the gifts she has been given—the gift of kindness, the gift of generosity, the gift of acceptance—and all of this translates into the gift of giving love, the very most important aspect of any human's life, but few know how to do it as well as you. Brenda, my child, let go, let go of your financial worries, knowing that I, your God, am here to protect you through all things. I, your God, will ensure you are taken care of. Know, my child, that I appreciate how hard you have worked to take care of yourself, but now I would like you to turn some of that over to me. Turn all that worry, all that fear, and all that anger over to me. As you have heard many times, I have big shoulders, and I can carry your stress much more efficiently than you can.

So, Brenda, this is what I ask of you: no more worrying, no more fretting, no more tears, knowing that I, your God, will take care of your problems. All I ask is that you continue to spread your love. You are so very, very good at that. And again, as you know, we should all do the things we are good at. So, my child, continue to spread your generosity, continue to spread your positive energy, and continue to spread that beautiful love of yours, knowing that I will take care of the rest. Give praise for all you have been given, give praise for the people in your life, and give praise that you are a favored child of God. Give praise, my child, and let me worry about the rest.

Your Loving God

Lord Jesus, do you have a message for me?

Yes Barbara, there is always a message waiting for you, a message of hope and love. You want to know more about the ego, let me tell you about the ego that you can teach others what to know about the ego.

The ego is created by insecurities that all humans suffer from; the insecurity of not being liked, the insecurity of making a mistake, the insecurity of not knowing something. The ego then takes these insecurities and builds them into something even bigger, something that isn't true and something that causes extreme stress to the body.

The ego is not from God but a learned behavior passed down through the generations. The ego deters a person from seeing the truth as it gets in the way of clarifying a situation and it gets in the way of being able to make a decision.

The ego is developed over the years of a person's life to protect that person, ironically the ego does not protect us at all but hinders us; hinders us from seeing the truth and hinders us from seeing others as they are. All is based on one's own needs and wants when we let the ego get in the way.

How do we learn to recognize the ego you ask? Well, when we make decisions on how we feel, when we react to others on how we feel, when we lash back because of how we feel. That is the ego.

We must consider our feelings but do not let them be involved in our reactions, do not let them be involved in our decision making. Feelings are to be taken into our safe places and discussed with God. Journal our feelings, share them with a trusted friend or write me a letter with all those feelings, share with your Lord and Savior. Take those feelings and put them in a special little box labelled my feelings, spend time with your feelings, analyze your feelings, just keep them out of decision making, reactions and discussions with people of influence.

Practice removing yourself from your ego. It will become easier to recognize what is the ego and what is the truth. Teach others Barb how to remove themselves from the ego and watch as people around you change. Watch as there is less confusion, watch as self- esteem grows and you will notice a different world around you. Practice the art of removing yourself from the ego and teach others to remove themselves from the ego.

Your Loving God

My dear Lord Jesus, sorry for the rant the other day and thank you for showing me what my true rewards are. Can you tell me about hell and what it is like. Thank you my Lord.

Dear Barbara,

You already know what hell is like, you are right, you have walked down the corridor of hell and never had to stay. But your Mother knew what hell was like when she had to live in a body that no longer works the way she wanted it to, a mind that cannot remember any more or articulate clear thoughts. Ask those people if it feels like hell to them. A place where you are no longer able to make a decision for yourself, all decision making is left to another human and not necessarily a human that really cares for you. Yes my child, that is hell.

Ask the addict, ask him what hell is like? Could it be a body trembling so bad you cannot hold your hand still but yet you still venture down a dark scary alley to try to find one more hit that will get you through the next hour. Does that feel like hell? Not knowing if ever there will be a time when you no longer need a chemical to get you through a day. Does that sound like hell?

What about the person that does not have anybody to love him, not a parent, not a sibling, not a friend? Yes my child, there really are people who do not have one single person to love them. Would that feel like hell?

There are many forms of hell right here on planet Earth and each of us has our own little piece of hell at some point in our life. Many of my children live in hell every day and all they really need is just one person to say, "hey man, how are you doing, is there anything at all I can do for you?"

Once again my child, it comes back to love. So when one of my creations does not feel love that is the definition of hell. When one of my creations cannot find the love they are looking for, that is hell.

Each of my children that are living in their own personal hell can move out of the location by extending love to someone, because as we send out love we get it back. As we extend grace, mercy and love it comes back to us. Those people who are caught up in their own personal hell are concentrating on themselves and have forgotten that many others also need attention.

Self-pity is a form of hell all in itself. What makes a person feel sadder or angrier than self-pity? Forget about self, forget about how bad you have it and look around- who can you help? Who would benefit from some love from you? Watch as everything changes for you. Help others and forgive others and you will glide out of the personal hell you have created for yourself.

The addict can help others; it does not always have to be about him. The infirmed can still bring joy to another with a smile or a light touch. The unloved can spread love to others more in need.

When we start to think of other people and how we might be able to make a difference in their lives is when we slip out of hell and onto the path that was meant for us. A path of joy, wonder, excitement and love available for everyone.

Once again my child, as you have heard many, many times each of my children was created to spread love, and when my children are spreading my love it is impossible to remain in hell. Move forward and continue to spread my love,

Your loving God.

My Precious Lord,

Today I need to ask about fairness in the world or more importantly about the unfairness in the world. I don't understand, there is so much to go around and yet there is a constant struggle in the world for so many to find enough to eat and others have so much, so much and yet it is not shared. As well those with so much seem to get more and those with so little seem to get less. This question isn't just about the wealth of the world it also pertains to the unfairness in every walk of life, what about the person who works so hard for a promotion and then the promotion is handed to the individual who seems to have just waltzed in and be handed the promotion.

Lord, wouldn't the world be a happier and a more productive place if all was fair, is it not possible for you to make the world fair?

Again my dear child, it is such a mystery to you that life is not fair, a mystery to you because you believe in fair, you believe in trust and you believe in love. Only in love will we see fairness, only in love will there ever be a change in greed. Greed is one of the deadly sins; greed is a personal fuel to feed the ego.

How do we talk about the ego in a way that helps you understand, how can we talk about the ego to bring awareness to the greed of the world for without the ego, the world would enjoy the fruits of the labor that brings a sense of love and responsibility to all, by all.

To understand the ego you first must understand the purpose and the learning of living on earth. The purpose and learning is to bring knowledge and growth to the soul, the soul learns through doing both what feels good and what feels bad. The soul has the ability to share the feelings of both good and bad which in turn can be an excellent tool for the body. When learning the life lessons of generosity it is a total alignment of the body, mind and soul. If just one is out of alignment you will begin to have the feelings of competition, greed and anger. However it is with the alignment of all three that creates the feelings of fairness.

Fairness you ask? How is fairness achieved in a world so full of unfairness, how can fairness be achieved when egos become challenged and left on their own to fight for their own? To fight for their own rights and privileges, rights and privileges that are held so close to the heart, rights and privileges that seem to come so seldom and when they appear they are coveted and protected to ensure their lasting value.

Generosity is a gift, a gift that few people possess. Generosity is one of the most precious gifts to possess because with generosity comes an open heart and an open heart is the healing essence of the world. When your heart is closed it is very hard to grow, it is very hard to change or better yourself. When the heart is open anything is possible.

Generosity comes in many forms, it can come in the form of offering a helping hand or a thoughtful word or even a gentle touch. Generosity is sharing what you have; generosity is a form of healing that brings great reward because when giving something you have to another you then begin the chain reaction of love, the universal language.

To help you understand better compare your own personal feelings, think of holding tightly to your money with fists clenched, now think of releasing your clenched fist and easily letting the money flow from your hands, and compare the two feelings. The first one of tightness and the second one of looseness, which one feels better?

And now you understand the difference between generosity and greed, it is not just a physical feeling it is also emotional as well as spiritual. Generosity is the personal feeling of freedom while greed is the personal feeling of restraint.

One heals the body while the other damages the body, now which one would you prefer?

BEV & BARB MUNRO

ABOUT THE AUTHOR

The authors of *Messages from Above* are identical twin sisters. Bev and Barb Munro were raised in a small city in Saskatchewan. Bev, who is older by fifteen minutes, moved to the city at seventeen years old, and Barb remained in their hometown. Both sisters are married and have three grown children and are now grandmas.

After taking a journaling class in 2000, Bev would practice the freedom writing technique often. One day, while journaling and writing a letter to God, she realized that she was receiving an answer to her questions. Ten years later, after much practice, Barb also was receiving answers to her questions.

Bev and Barb have put a few of these letters into a book so others can benefit from the messages from above they have received.

You may contact them at bevandbarbmunro@gmail.com